PRAISE FOR
CALL A THING A THING

Adam Aziz has hit the mark with this book! Change can only take place when we decide to live accountable and "do the work" to place our lives on a higher trajectory. It is without hesitation that I endorse this book. I'm going to "call a thing a thing" … Adam has done the work! We really can live empowered!

PASTOR REITA BALL

CO-FOUNDER & CO-PASTOR
OF METRO TAB CHURCH
CHATTANOOGA, TN
WWW.METROTAB.NET

If you feel stuck or simply feel like you're not where you want to be then **you have to read this book.** *Call A Thing A Thing* is a powerful read and full of facts. This book brings about perspective shifts that will shift your trajectory.

**PASTOR KIM JONES
"REAL TALK KIM"**

FOUNDER OF
CONQUERING HELL
IN HIGH HEELS, INC.
WWW.REALTALKKIM.COM

Adam Aziz very clearly and practically tells the reader how to affect change in their life through the power of the Holy Spirit. *Call A Thing A Thing* is the best God centered self-help book I have ever read.

BOB LUBELL

PRESIDENT AND FOUNDER OF
PARTNERS FOR CHRISTIAN MEDIA

Check out this new book from my good friend, Adam Aziz! **It will push you to a new level** in Christ! This book will empower you to look at your life, tell the truth, and trust God through the process!

ADAM CRABB

RECORDING ARTIST
GATHER VOCAL BAND
THE CRABB FAMILY
WWW.ADAMCRABB.COM

This book is everything you didn't know you needed to hear. Adam shares such incredible insight and motivation, but most of all truth. This book will both inspire you as well as correct wrong thinking. This isn't a "self-help" book, those only make you feel good. No, **this book is healing medicine for your soul.** What you'll find as you dive into this well thought out and strategic book is the discovery of truth gets more revealing and intense the further you read. Some parts will not feel good, but that's the point. Make no mistake, you will be better when you are bold enough to call a thing a thing.

PASTOR DEVON GOINS

LIFE.CHURCH WORSHIP
WWW.LIFE.CHURCH

Call A Thing A Thing releases you to be you in raw truth. This book will encourage you to seek God for His plan and empower you to accept no counterfeit definitions of yourself. **Truth becomes your best friend.**

ANGELA PRIMM

ANGELA PRIMM MINISTRIES
AUTHOR OF
SO YOU SAY YOU WANT TO SING
WWW.ANGELAPRIMM.COM

Adam Aziz's book *Call A Thing A Thing* is such a timely word, especially in a generation of political correctness where people are afraid to speak the truth in love. In this book, **Adam Aziz graciously and strategically drops truth bomb after truth bomb in a way that helps realign the heart posture and build character and integrity in our lives.** This book is written in a simple and easy to read style that brings out fresh and brilliant timeless truths to our daily lives. I highly recommend this book to every person who longs for an authentic relationship with God and desires to grow deeper in their character and integrity.

DR. CHARLES KARUKU

REVIVALIST AND PRESIDENT OF
UNITY REVIVAL MOVEMENT
MINNEAPOLIS, MN

Adam Aziz has written a book that has the potential to bring freedom into anyone's life who reads it. No psychobabble here. The truth of God's Word is enough to free us from the tyranny of ourselves. I plan to use this book as a companion resource in counseling folks to wholeness. Clearly written and to the point, *Call A Thing A Thing* **is our God's blueprint for freedom.**

DR. SHIRLEY ARNOLD

AUTHOR OF RELEVANCE
APOSTLE AT
THE REVIVAL PEOPLE NETWORK

We live in times when truth is not only relative but also a rare commodity. As I turned the pages of *Call A Thing A Thing* by Adam Aziz, **I realized how valuable the words of this book are for our social media, filter covered and virtual reality generation.** Finally, we have a clarion call for a return to truth for every husband, wife, pastor, church leader, member or anyone trying to find their true north.

PASTOR EVANS KARIUKI

FOUNDER OF FIREBRAND NATION
PASTOR OF
ETERNAL LIFE HARVEST CENTER
AUTHOR OF FIREBRAND
WWW.ELHC.LIFE

The notion that time heals all things simply is not true regarding mental and spiritual issues. The only way to heal pain of this nature is to face and confront it. Adam Aziz encourages us how to confront ourselves in his book, *Call A Thing A Thing*. From identification to mastery, Adam uses scripture and personal testimony to motivate the reader through the process to freedom in Christ. While personal growth insists on bravery and multi-layered confrontation, **you will visit the information found in this book time and again to hone in on your God-given peace, integrity, and destiny.**

JEFF TAYLOR

FOUNDER OF
TAYLOR MINISTRIES
WWW.TAYLORMINISTRIES.COM

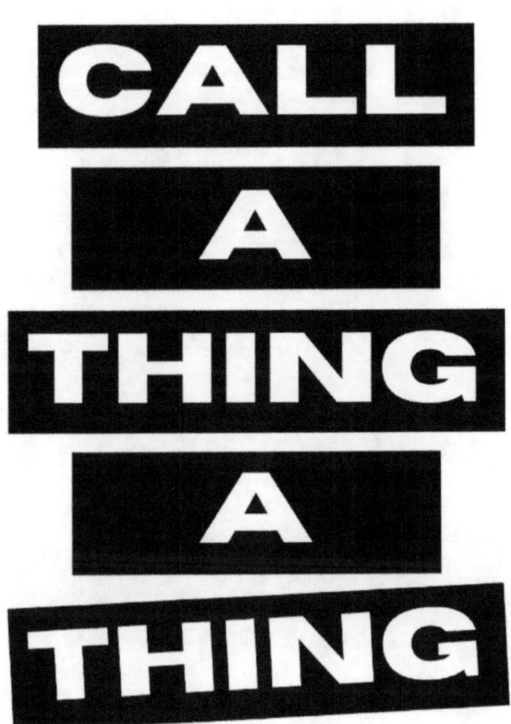
CALL
A
THING
A
THING

FOREWORD
DR. STEVE BALL

In his insightful book, "Call A Thing A Thing," Adam Aziz captures the essence of being honest with oneself. This fresh new look at self-examination causes you to evaluate actions, motives, and purpose. If we are to reach our full potential, we must live by basic principles of integrity with ourselves.

In a day when fake news is the order of the day and the internet is a top choice for information, even the most discerning people are often misled. Besides having to sort through false information we must avoid making excuses when it is easier to do so than it is to face reality.

Adam Aziz presses the reader to see it straight and call it straight while he outlines step by step instructions on how to call things as they are and make it happen. In doing so, he pushes the reader to make wise choices, follow through with important plans and succeed while moving to the next level.

This process of receiving excellent instruction, orchestrating strategic plans, and following up on actions attempted and completed are an excellent recipe for success. Adam Aziz leads by example. It has been my privilege to watch him develop his leadership skills and put them into practice for many years. His success speaks for itself.

This book is a must read for those diligent about personal growth and development. Adam is a model leader that exemplifies excellence in everything he does. The principles laid out in this book will assist those serious about their own personal growth and development as well as help them become excellent leaders.

In an ever-changing society, multiple cultural inequities, and an age of deception, it is more imperative than ever to "Call A Thing A Thing" as part of your daily journey. Start now by learning how to do exactly that in every area of your life.

Dr. Steve Ball
Lead Pastor of Metro Tab Church
www.metrotab.net

ADAM AZIZ

FOREWORD BY: DR. STEVE BALL

HONESTY IS THE PLACE WHERE BREAKTHROUGH HAPPENS.

Call A Thing A Thing

Proverbs 18:22 (ESV)
"He who finds a wife finds a good thing
and obtains favor from the Lord."

*To my wife who keeps me honest and always encourages me to tell
the truth – thank you for allowing God to use you to change my life.
You are the best thing in my life and because of you, I know I have
received favor from the Lord!*

CONTENTS

ONE

EASIER SAID THAN DONE

...Don't think you are better than you really are.
Be honest in your evaluation of yourselves...
Romans 12:3 (NLT)

CALLING A "THING" A "THING" is something we all must do in our lives if we are ever truly going to live free. Jesus said in John 8:32, *"You will know the truth, and the truth will make you free"* (ERV). When you choose to look right at a "thing", acknowledge its existence, call it exactly by its name, and then decide what role it will play in your life, you have just chosen to take the first step toward freedom. We all have "things" in our lives whether they are inherited through family generations or produced by our choices. Some of us have more "things" than others. It's easier said than done to call our "things" exactly what they are without sugar coating or dressing them up to look pretty. This book will challenge your assumptions, abilities, thoughts, and everything in between to interrupt your story and teach you how to call a "thing" a "thing." Will it be easy? No! Will it be worth it? Absolutely!

Admitting the truth and confronting yourself with the hard conversations about your life is never easy. I have found many people want to be a diamond, but very few are willing to get cut. Many people want to be a diamond, but very few want to go through the process of becoming a diamond. Diamonds are made 100 miles deep within the Earth. Diamonds are made in temperatures boiled above 2,000 degrees fahrenheit and pressure exceeding 725,000 pounds per square inch. People want to be diamonds, but they do not want to be hidden, they cannot stand the heat, and they cannot handle the pressure. It's always easier to point the finger at others than to embrace positive change in your own life. I have learned from my own personal experiences that if I do not call what I am feeling or thinking by its actual name I give it power over my life. It is easy to call the hurt you are feeling and the negative responses it makes you have, "defending yourself". It is easier to make excuses for your bad behavior or even shift the blame and point the finger at someone else rather than owning your feelings or the contribution you made to the break down in a relationship.

Mislabeling a "thing" is lying about a "thing." When you mislabel you are lying to yourself and all who are involved. If you're not a liar, stop telling lies. Honor God, others, and yourself enough to walk in the truth. This book is about empowering you to tell the truth. Tell the truth about your relationships. Tell the truth about your behavior. Tell the truth about your dysfunction, confusion, fear, and insecurities. Tell the truth about your past and your present. Tell the truth about your life and your choices.

The truth is the only safe ground to stand on.

The Apostle Paul said, "...*Don't think you are better than you really are. Be honest in your evaluation of yourselves...*" (Romans 12:3, NLT). Once something is accurately identified and the truth is told, you have built a foundation for the wisdom, integrity, and the understanding to find healing and peace. It is time to tell the truth and call a "thing" a "thing."

WHAT IS CALLING A "THING" A "THING?"

Calling a "thing" a "thing" is simply telling the truth. The only way to stay in peace and integrity within ourselves is to tell the truth. It can be hard. It can be difficult. It may scare you. It may offend you. For these reasons we delete information, embellish and stretch the story, or we avoid the issue altogether. Then before you know it that "thing" has blown up in your face and you wonder, "Why?" We cover our personal issues and struggles with lies to make us feel better about the reality of our current state. This act is mental, emotional, and spiritual suicide; because if we continue to deny and tell lies, we will never heal. Nor will we ever grow or go to a new level of living. When you do not tell the truth, the lie controls your life. We must tell the truth, especially about ourselves. I have learned this truth…

If you continue to argue against reality, you will suffer.

Calling a "thing" a "thing" empowers you to break the cycle of negativity and create new, positive patterns for your life. Telling the truth about every aspect of our lives is the only way we can progress or move forward on our journey. I believe that the journey is not so much about becoming anything. The journey is about unbecoming everything that is not really you so you can be who you were meant to be. It is imperative to tell the truth about what you are feeling, thinking, doing, and why you are doing it. When you tell the truth to yourself about yourself, you bring yourself into alignment with God's purpose and plan for your life.

When you call a "thing" a "thing", you embrace healing and breakthrough; you take your life back from any brokenness or bitterness that has settled in your heart. Healing hurts, and to experience real breakthrough, something must break. It is like resetting a bone that has healed in the wrong position. Everything may look okay on the outside, but you have lost the full functionality of that bone; you have crippled, limited, and disabled yourself. For everything to return to proper alignment, you have to re-break the bone and start the healing process all over again. The process hurts, but in the end, you have given yourself the full ability and freedom to pursue life without the limitations of brokenness.

Sometimes things that seem so easy are much harder to do. The idea of calling a "thing" a "thing" is simple. Telling the truth seems easy enough, but doing it is a little more complicated. Naming your "thing" requires the humility to admit the truth of how you got there. No matter how hard it is, it must happen. It is the greatest service you could do for yourself. Your life, your happiness, and your healing are depending on it. The key is to keep a positive attitude. When it gets difficult you must remember that nothing worth having comes easy because what comes easy will not last and what lasts will not come easy. When it starts getting tough, that means you are on the verge of breakthrough.

EMBRACE YOUR NEW SEASON

You were created to be more. You are entitled to the best that life has to offer. God wants you to be in a better place mentally, emotionally, relationally, and spiritually. God does not want you to simply exist or get by. He wants you to experience all that He has for you in this life. God has a plan, a purpose, and a destiny for your life. In Jeremiah 29:11 the Lord declares, *"'For I know the plans I have for you," says the Lord. "They are plans for good and not for disaster, to give you a future and a hope'"* (NLT). If your life is not exceptional, plentiful, and powerful you are living beneath the privilege that God has for you. God's desire is that you live a good and blessed life that is filled with favor and outrageous joy.

God's love for you is unconditional and limitless. Which means, even though He can see the worst in you, He still wants the best for you. The question is, do **YOU** want the best life you can possibly live? If so, then tell the truth. Where you have been does not have to determine where you are going. What you have experienced does not have the power to determine how you feel, think, or live. You are not the total of your bad experiences. When you mess up you must own it and clear it quickly. Once you start telling lies and denying your role in the story, denial becomes a way of life. Before you know it, you don't know who you are or how you got there. The first part of your story may be a horror story, but it's time to embrace a new season, interrupt the story, and call a "thing" a "thing."

WHERE YOU
HAVE BEEN
DOES NOT
HAVE TO
DETERMINE
WHERE YOU
ARE GOING.

____

Embracing a new season requires you to know who you are. Who you are is not your name, your occupation, or even what people say or think about you. Who you are is something wonderful and powerful. Who you are is someone God can use to make a difference in the earth. Who you are is someone God can use to make someone else's life better. Who you are is someone God can use to create effective and lasting change in the world. When you don't know who you are you get stuck with all of your limited perceptions.

Embracing a new season requires your behavior to align with who you know you are. If you're not a mean and wicked person; you don't act like a mean and wicked person. If you're not a dead-beat daddy; you don't act like a dead-beat daddy. If you're not a cheater and a sneak; you don't cheat, and you don't sneak. You must start behaving like who you are. If you are a friend; behave like a friend. If you are a father; behave like a father. If you are a leader; behave like a leader. Your behavior is a demonstration of what you believe about yourself. Your behavior demonstrates who you are.

Embracing a new season requires you to put yourself first. It is not selfish to put yourself first. Putting yourself first does not mean you disregard others. To help someone else, you must come to them with your cup full and running over. What comes out of the cup is for other people, but what is in the cup is yours. You matter.

Embracing a new season requires you to not accept the unacceptable. You do not have to be broke. You do not have to struggle. You do not have to be sad and sorry. Be willing to do a new thing and go a new way. You may make some people mad in the process. People will hold you to your limitations. People will hold you to what they believe to be true about you. Do not sit around believing that because it has not happened it will not happen. Do not believe the lie that says that because it has always happened it has to continue to happen. Do not accommodate and tolerate the things that do not honor the truth of who you are.

Embracing a new season requires you to change your thinking. In Proverbs 23:7 we read, *"For as he thinks in his heart, so is he..."* (NKJV). You are what you think. If you think you're defeated, you will always be defeated. If you think things won't change, you will never see anything change. If you think there is no hope, you will never find hope. You are the product of your thinking. If you can change the way you think you can change your life!

Embracing a new season requires you to unpack the baggage. We all carry around baggage. The baggage we carry can be good and it can be bad. The baggage we carry can be something we have gained from past life experiences or something that we have inherited. We all have baggage, and our baggage holds us back from reaching our destiny. For example: each person is allowed a certain number of bags on an airplane flight. There are fees for extra baggage. What am I saying? I'm saying that the more baggage you have the greater the cost to get where you're going. Check your baggage, unpack it, and only carry the necessities with you.

Embracing a new season requires you to ask for what you want. James 4:2 teaches us that, *"...You don't get what you want because you don't ask God..."* (ERV). Do not settle for what's available or for what you think you can get. Ask God for what you want and aim high. Accept only things that are going to raise the bar in your life. This is God's desire for you!

Embracing a new season requires you to be grounded spiritually. This means that every day when you wake up and your feet hit the floor you connect with, believe in, and trust in God the Father. If you don't, you can be knocked down by anything that comes your way. In Colossians 2:6-7, the Apostle Paul says, *"And now, just as you accepted Christ Jesus as your Lord, you must continue to follow Him. Let your roots grow down into Him, and let your lives be built on Him. Then your faith will grow strong in the truth you were taught, and you will overflow with thankfulness"* (NLT).

GOD OR YOUR EGO?

Calling a "thing" a "thing" is easier said than done, but it can be done. Yes! Life is hard, healing hurts, moving forward is scary, and telling the truth isn't fun but these things can be done. The question is, will you do it? When things get uncomfortable, we create excuses to avoid having to deal with it. It's a pride issue. Telling the truth is so hard because we do not want to humble ourselves enough to admit our truth, to name our "thing". So, we cover it up. We think, "If I don't have to tell the truth or hear the truth, I don't have to change." The bottom line is this: Who will win the battle? **GOD** or your **EGO**? Because…

E.G.O. **E**ases **G**od **O**ut!

Ego never accepts the truth. God is calling you to tell the truth so that you can be the best version of yourself. Be willing to have the hard conversations with yourself and confront your issues. Do the work that feeds your soul and not your ego. Often, our problems are the result of our choices. Look at conflict as an opportunity to move toward a resolution and healing. It's very simple: when the voice of **EGO** speaks, tell it to shut up. Everybody has a "thing" whether it is: meanness, bitterness, un-forgiveness, resistance, arrogance, trauma, ego, rebelliousness, an experience that you can't let go of, a belief, a behavior, a way of being, or something else. The first step is calling it by its name. Once you call your "thing" a "thing", you can give it a place in your life, or you can dismiss it and let it go.

It's time to be powerful not pitiful. My hope is that as you read you will be inspired and empowered to lay aside mediocrity, to live your life with excellence, and to pursue your destiny. I hope this book challenges you to re-think your life choices. All of this might be easier said than done, but the thing is, it can be done! It's time to deal with your problems: face them, confess them, understand what they are, and where they came from; this is the process. Let's go to work!

TWO

DO YOUR WORK

Do not despise these small beginnings,
for the Lord rejoices to see the work begin...
Zechariah 4:10a (NLT)

work: |wərk| - *verb*
exerting oneself physically or mentally to do, make or accomplish something; arriving at a specified condition through gradual or repeated movement; proceeding or progressing slowly and laboriously; undergoing small motions that result in friction and wear; cultivating

Let's break down the meaning of "doing your work". For you to accomplish change, to make a difference in your life, to reach your life goals, or to find breakthrough and healing you are going to have to do the work. The change, healing, and breakthrough we are all so desperately seeking in our lives will not happen overnight; it is a gradual, daily, laborious effort. You may experience some friction, wear, and agitation, but through the process you will find God cultivating you into a powerful person.

Doing the work means doing what is necessary and required to know the truth of who you are and the best of who you are. Doing the work is looking at those places that keep you from being authentic – who you were destined to be. Doing the work is confronting those things that keep you from being the best of who you are – who God has created you to be. I am talking about giving yourself permission to look at the unveiled truth inside of you. When I say, "do the work", I'm saying, be with yourself for a minute. Sit down, be quiet, and listen. Go to the places that scare you and make you uncomfortable. Go to the places where you hurt and understand what that hurt is, its origin, and what you need to do to eliminate it. Go to the places where you don't like yourself. Each of us has something we do not like about ourselves. Go to that place. What are the things you were told that you cannot do and therefore have never bothered to try? We accept limitations that people put on us and we never question or challenge them. Maybe you really can sing. Maybe you really can write. Maybe you really can dance. Have you done the necessary work to explore, investigate, and discover your possibilities?

Who wants to do the work? None of us do. We don't want to work. We want to play and have fun. With our busy, fast-passed society, we want things to be quick and easy. We don't want to do the difficult stuff. But when it comes to living, learning, and growing, the "work" refers to what you have to do within yourself to be the person you were created and destined to be – to live your best life. The work means understanding what you do, how you do it, why you do it, and what you get as the result. Everybody's work is different. Some of us must work on our actions. Some of us must work on our thoughts. Some of us must work on our feelings. Regardless, everyone must do the work on the areas that create negativity, confusion, dysfunction, chaos, conflict, or failure in his or her life. We must do the work within ourselves to clean it up. Every thought you have and every word you speak matters. Thoughts and words have power. Once you think it and once you speak it, it exists. Therefore, it is important to do the work that will root out any negative thing you might be harboring.

You can start small! Doing your work doesn't mean going in with a wrecking ball and doing a massive overhaul of your life. You can begin making changes in your life, brick by brick. Zechariah 4:10a says, "*Do not*

YOU CAN BEGIN MAKING CHANGES IN YOUR LIFE, BRICK BY BRICK.

despise these small beginnings, for the Lord rejoices to see the work begin..." (NLT). God does not expect a "new you" to appear overnight. He is simply happy to see you doing the work, caring enough about the life He has given you to start making a change.

ABIDE THROUGH THE PRUNING

Doing your work begins with allowing God to work on you. Walking in the spirit and in the Word of God opens us up to the fullness of God to be made manifest in our daily lives. It produces healthy growth and abundant fruit. When God made you, He designed you to run at the optimal level. You can be supernaturally filled with the fullness of God.

The Apostle Paul said, "*I pray that from His glorious, unlimited resources He will empower you with inner strength through His Spirit. Then Christ will make His home in your hearts as you trust in Him. Your roots will grow down into God's love and keep you strong. And may you have the power to understand, as all God's people should, how wide, how long, how high, and how deep His love is. May you experience the love of Christ, though it is too great to understand fully. Then you will be made complete with all the fullness of life and power that comes from God. Now all glory to God, who is able, through His mighty power* **at work within us**, *to accomplish infinitely more than we might ask or think*" (Ephesians 3:16-20 NLT). To be full of God is to be full of everything God has for you. To be full of God is to be full of His love, peace, power, favor, blessings, and joy. To be filled with the fullness of God, we must allow His Spirit and His Word to be **at work** in us.

When God is at work in us, we must *abide* through the process if we want to see healthy and abundant fruit produced in our lives. When God's Word and His Spirit begin working in you, you will be equipped and empowered to work on yourself, and effect change in your life. We cannot do the work on our own; we need Him.

Jesus said in John 15:1-8, "'*I am the true vine, and My Father is the vinedresser. Every branch in Me that does not bear fruit He takes away;*

*and every branch that bears fruit He **prunes**, that it may bear more fruit. You are already clean because of the word which I have spoken to you. **Abide** in Me, and I in you. As the branch cannot bear fruit of itself, unless it abides in the vine, neither can you, unless you abide in Me. "I am the vine; you are the branches. He who abides in Me, and I in him, bears much fruit; **for without Me you can do nothing.** If anyone does not abide in Me, he is cast out as a branch and is withered; and they gather them and throw them into the fire, and they are burned. If you abide in Me, and My words abide in you, you will ask what you desire, and it shall be done for you. By this My Father is glorified, that you bear much fruit; so, you will be My disciples"* (NKJV).

We must abide in the vine. Jesus said in John 15:1-2, *" 'I am the true vine, and My Father is the vinedresser. Every branch in Me that does not bear fruit He takes away; and every branch that bears fruit He **prunes**, that it may bear more fruit"* (NKJV).

prune: |pro͞on| - *verb*
to rid of impurities; to cleanse; to purify; to free; to remove
by cleansing or purifying; to eliminate; to empty

You cannot be filled with the fullness of God unless you are first emptied! We must be emptied of anger, hate, fear, bitterness, un-forgiveness, sin, ego, and whatever else is filling us. Until you are emptied you can never be filled. Until you are purged you can never be abundant. Until you are pruned you can never be fruitful. Until God works on you, you cannot do the work.

Once you attach yourself to the vine (Jesus), the Vinedresser (God) comes in and begins **pruning** the branches (You). Pruning is a practice involving the selective removal of parts of a plant, such as branches, buds, or roots. Reasons to prune plants include deadwood removal, shaping (by controlling or directing growth), improving or maintaining health, reducing risk from falling branches, and both harvesting and increasing the yield or quality of fruits. The practice entails targeted removal of diseased, damaged, dead, non-productive, structurally unsound, or otherwise unwanted tissue from crop and landscape plants.

When the Holy Spirit begins working on your life, pruning you, He will target the diseased and dead things in your life such as wrong thinking or living in the past. He will remove the damaged things in your life such as bitterness and hurt feelings. He will target the removal of the structurally unsound relationships and the destructive choices in your life. Why does He do this? So that He can shape and direct your growth. He prunes you so that He can improve and maintain your mental, emotional, and spiritual health. He works in your life so that you can produce quality fruit.

After He tells you that you are going to be pruned, He says that you must *abide*. Jesus said in John 15:4, "**Abide** *in Me, and I in you. As the branch cannot bear fruit of itself, unless it abides in the vine, neither can you, unless you abide in Me...*" (NKJV).

> **a·bide:** |ə ˈbīd| - *verb*
> to put up with; to tolerate; to endure; to wait patiently for; to remain in a place; to dwell; to submit; to accept without opposition or question; to remain faithful; to stand; to suffer

We must put up with and tolerate the work and the process God does in our lives. We must remain in position, endure, and submit to God's working in our lives. We must remain faithful to God and to the process of making changes and doing the work, even when it hurts. We must accept the truth about ourselves without opposition, resistance, or question. Why? Because without God's truth, His Word, and His Spirit working in our lives, the work we do on ourselves will be in vain.

I am reminded of the Apostle Paul whose name was once Saul. He was originally known for persecuting and killing Christians. He attached himself to the vine (Jesus), and he knew how to abide. Despite His past, reputation, and bad behavior, he was able to write more of the New Testament than any other person; he touched more territory with the Gospel than any other person in His time. When we abide, God can work in us to produce much fruit. Jesus said in John 15:5, "*I am the vine, you are the branches. He who abides in Me, and I in him, bears much fruit;* **for without Me you can do nothing**..." (NLT). It is important that we realize that without abiding through the process and God's help, doing the work is impossible.

YOUR PROGRESS IS IN THE PROCESS

Once God begins His work in you, you can begin working on yourself. Doing your work is a process.

proc·ess: |ˌprä ̣ses, ˈprō ̣ses|
noun. a series of actions that produce a *change* or development; *changes* or functions bringing about a result; progress; – *verb.* a forward movement

Process isn't fun. In Daniel chapter two we see that God changes the times and the seasons. God places us in a season of process to bring forth the change we want to see in our lives. He does this because He is trying to develop your character. He is trying to take you forward into something new. Your progress is in your process.

Do you want to progress in life? Do you want to grow? If the answer is - "yes", then you are going to have to endure the process. You are going to have to embrace and accept *change*. When things change you have two choices; you can either change with them *(be flexible)* or get out of the way. Stop being a stumbling block in your own life! We point the finger at others and blame everybody else, but we are the ones in the way of our own progress. You must do your work.

THREE STEPS

There are three steps for doing the work. These three steps are the way you obtain personal inner healing and breakthrough. Taking these three steps moves you forward…

1. Acknowledge. You must acknowledge what you do. The good behavior and the bad behavior. Everybody has a "thing", and you must acknowledge it. You must call a "thing" a "thing." What is your thing? Your thing is that nasty, ugly, mean thing you do instead of acknowledging, "I made a mistake. I messed up. I didn't do what I was supposed to do."

Acknowledgement is the first step. You cannot change what you will not acknowledge.

2. Accept. Accept that there are some parts of you that need healing, growing, stretching, or changing. There are some things in you that are beautiful and things that are ugly. There are parts of you that are powerful and parts of you that are pitiful. If you do not acknowledge it, you cannot accept it. If you do not accept it, you cannot heal it. Everybody has a "thing" that they do, a way that they act, a habit, or a belief that shows up in certain situations. What is your thing? Acknowledge it and accept it.

3. Abort. If you do not sacrifice for what you want, what you want becomes the sacrifice. After you acknowledge and accept those "things", abort them. Get rid of them. Change them. Then, go for your best life! The way you go for your best life is you trust your source, the Creator, your Maker, God. You must trust that power within you that makes you, your thoughts, and your words powerful. 1 John 4:4 says, *"You are of God, little children, and have overcome them, because He who is in you is greater than he who is in the world"* (NKJV). Trust that! Stand on that! He will push you out of your comfort zone. He will take you out of the known and put you in the unknown. He will take you from ordinary to extraordinary and from mediocre to magnificent. We can stand on the promise that Jesus made in Matthew 19:26, *"...With man this is impossible, but with God all things are possible"* (NIV).

LEARN TO ACCEPT FAILURE, NOT DEFEAT

You must do your work. You may have messed up in life. You may have created bad habits and accepted negative cycles. You may have even behaved badly, but that is not the end of your story. It does not have to define your future or determine where you're going. Yes, you may have messed up. Learn to accept that truth. Learn to accept that you may have failed. Never accept that you are defeated. The voice of defeat is a lie. The voice that tells you that things will never turn around is a lie. The voice that tells you that you can never change and that it is too difficult, is a lie. When those voices speak tell them to **SHUT UP!**

You can start again. Believe that! Stand in that truth. You don't have to start over. You can simply start again. When a train derails, it is put right back on the track at the place of derailment. That's right, you can start right where you got off track. First you must identify where and why you derailed and start rebuilding. You can get your life back on the right track, but you must do your work! We must remember that there are two things we are in complete control of in our lives, our attitude and our effort. It's time to work on **YOU**.

THREE

THE RISE OF RESISTANCE

For the desires of the flesh are against the Spirit,
and the desires of the Spirit are against the flesh,
for these are opposed to each other, to keep you
from doing the things you want to do.
Galatians 5:17 (ESV)

Contrary to popular belief, we are not programmed to hate change. In fact, we like change. We change our hair styles and color. We rearrange our furniture. We change out our clothes. We change jobs. We change churches. We like change. What people don't like is how you try to change them. We like change on our terms. We like change when it makes us feel good or look good. The moment changing requires us to do something we don't like or that doesn't make us feel good, we resist it. Why? What causes this resistance?

Resistance is a response produced by our flesh. Its agenda is to distract us from doing our work and producing positive change in our lives. It discourages us from working on ourselves. In Galatians 5:17 we read, *"For the desires of the flesh are against the Spirit, and the desires of the Spirit are against the flesh, for these are opposed to each other, to keep you from doing the things you want to do"* (ESV). We want to change. We want to be better and do better. We want to grow and to heal. We want to become the best version of ourselves. However, when the time comes to tell the truth and do the work required, resistance starts rising. Let me be clear. Resistance does not come from the devil. Resistance comes from you – your flesh. Don't blame the devil for the acts of your flesh. We are not dealing with the devil; we will deal with him later. Right now, we are dealing with YOU.

Jesus said in Matthew 26:41, *"Pray for strength against temptation. Your spirit wants to do what is right, but your flesh is weak"* (NLT). We must pray that the desires of the Spirit are strengthened in us so that we do not fall to the flesh. The Spirit wants to empower you to do better and live on a higher level. The flesh is weak, and it's lazy. It does not want to do the work. The flesh resists.

Resistance may seem harmless, but be not deceived, your resistance does not want to wound or disable; it wants to kill. Resistance is a self-destructive, self-sabotaging act of our flesh. Let's look at how resistance operates in our lives…

Resistance will seduce and fabricate. Resistance takes on any form to deceive you. When you are driven by resistance you will willfully lie to yourself about your problems. Resistance will try to "logically" trick you into believing a lie. For example: Your friend, because they care about you, reveals a behavior that is potentially fatal to your future. If you are resistant to their revelation, you will fabricate lies that will validate your refusal to make lasting change. Instead of acknowledging that there is work to be done to better yourself, you will tell yourself that your friend is jealous of you, doesn't care about you, or is picking on you.

Resistance will distract. That's its goal. You know that you're lying to yourself when you look for distractions so that you can avoid the real stuff, the hard problems, and the truth. You distract yourself instead of working on the issues in your life. Do not forget the process for dealing with your problems: face them, confess them, and understand what they are. At some point you must ask yourself the question, "What is my contribution to the dysfunction in my life?" then face and accept the truth.

What happens when you lie about your problems? You suffer. That's right. If you argue against reality you will suffer. Lying about your problem sets you up for infection rather than healing. It is very easy to lie and deny the facts about your "thing". It is easy to throw a band-aide on it and hope for the best. Once you start lying about your problem you create a pattern of lying and denial in your life. Our intentions for lying to ourselves are not bad. In fact, we lie to ourselves because we seek comfort, but comfort is overrated. We want to believe our lie because if we consider the truth, it could hurt our ego. Just like pouring alcohol on a wound, it may sting at first, but telling the truth is the only thing that can truly clean your problem and set you up for healing.

Resistance will falsify the facts. You will begin inventing or concocting excuses for your bad behavior. You will twist and distort the narrative. You will find yourself shifting blame and pointing your finger at everyone else but **YOU**. To do your work effectively, you must stop talking about what "they" did and start talking about what **YOU** did. Stop looking at everyone else and look at yourself. Most of our problems have been created by our choices. Change your choices. Choose to admit and own the role you played in the story. We all play a role in the story. You played a role in that misunderstanding. You played a role in that relationship breakdown. Own it. Maybe you did not communicate clearly. Maybe you did not understand the situation fully. Maybe you behaved badly. It doesn't make you a bad person. It just makes you human. So, own it. Behavior is a symptom. We must get to the cause. Until you get to the cause of the pain, you cannot heal the pain and make it go away. Until you first get to the cause of your bad behavior, you cannot change it. Remember, you will never see new fruit until you first deal with the root.

If you aren't careful you will begin to believe the lies you told to cover up your "thing". You will believe the excuses you created for your bad behavior. The only way to break the destructive cycles created by

YOU WILL NEVER SEE NEW FRUIT UNTIL YOU FIRST DEAL WITH THE ROOT.

---

resistance is to "walk by the Spirit". The Apostle Paul teaches in Galatians 5:16 and 24-25, "*...walk by the Spirit, and you will not gratify the desires of the flesh. Those who belong to Christ Jesus have crucified the flesh with its passions and desires. If we live by the Spirit, let us also walk by the Spirit*" (ESV).

Paul told us that we are to *"crucify the flesh with its passions and desires."* This reminds me of the example set by Jesus at the crucifixion. Jesus did not simply die on the cross for our sin. Jesus is our example. He died to show us how to die. You must choose to crucify the flesh and submit to the Spirit of God in your life each day. Jesus set a great example of this in the garden of Gethsemane before His death and resurrection. He said in Luke 22:42, *"Father, if You are willing, please take this cup of suffering away from me. But I want Your will to be done, not mine*" (NLT). The will of His flesh was not to endure the pain, humiliation, disgrace, and suffering of the cross, but He endured it. Why? Because He was submitted to the will of God in His life. Submission is bringing your mission under the mission or authority of another person. Jesus made His flesh submit to the Spirit. He put the mission of His will and His flesh under the mission or authority of God. The mission of His flesh was not to endure the pain, but the mission of the Spirit was that He endure the cross so that you and I could live forgiven and free! I am so thankful He submitted! How about you?

What does it mean to walk by the Spirit? It means allowing the Word of God to be a lamp that guides your steps, a light that shows the path you should take. It means not being led by the emotional reactions of the flesh but applying the principles taught in the scriptures to your everyday living. It means not being driven by every thought that pops into your head but making those thoughts submit to the Spirit. Jesus said in John 8:31-32, *"If you live out what I teach you, then you will experience for yourselves the truth, and the truth will free you*" (MSG). The Apostle Paul said in 2 Timothy 3:16-17, "*All Scripture is inspired by God and is useful to teach us what is true and to make us realize what is wrong in our lives. It corrects us when we are wrong and teaches us to do what is right. God uses it to prepare and equip His people to do **every good work**"* (NLT). God's Word is where you begin to do the work. His Word will produce wisdom in you which will prepare you to make better choices for your life. His Word will empower and equip you to make positive changes. It will shift your way of thinking, causing vibrant and healthy fruit to be produced in your life. His Word will help you face the truth.

Is any of this easy? Of course not. That's why it's called, "work". Give yourself permission to be better than you currently are. The way you do that is to simply choose. It is an everyday choice we must all make.

CHOOSE WISELY

You need to make, even change, some choices to successfully do your work. Your choices will make or break your destiny. People, life circumstances, nor anything else have the power to determine who you are or where you are going. Your choices have that kind of power.

Choice is a right and a power given to us from God. You reap the consequences of your choices. Your choices are the essential ingredient of the manifestation of all habits, conditions, judgments, limitations, and beliefs that you have. They are the cornerstone of all success and failure in your life. Therefore, it is crucial that you never make a permanent decision in a temporary situation.

Every experience we have faced or will ever face in life is a result of our choices; choices made, and choices resisted. The Lord told the children of Israel in Deuteronomy 30:19a, "*Today I am giving you a choice of two ways. And I ask heaven and earth to be witnesses of your choice. You can choose life or death. The first choice will bring a blessing. The other choice will bring a curse. So, choose life!*" (ERV). You may have heard the saying, "Life is a test." If it is a test, it is an open book test! The answer is right in front of you. **CHOOSE**. Choose life. The choice is yours. Which will you choose?

Today, you can choose to do the work. You can choose to walk in the truth. You can choose to walk in freedom. You can choose to live whole and in peace. You can choose to **LIVE**! Until the choice to do the work is made, you will live your life set on default, living as a victim of circumstances, and accepting whatever happens in your life. When you make the conscious choice to work on yourself, you become empowered. You become empowered to live a blessed life, a life filled with love, joy, and peace. Choose that today! When resistance rises, push it aside. Then face the hard truth and choose to embrace real change. Your future will be glad you did!

FOUR

TRUST THE PROCESS

Here is my advice:
It would be good for you to finish what you started…
2 Corinthians 8:10-12 (NLT)

There are dreams, aspirations, and goals that God places in our hearts and He gives them to us right away. Often, He does not give them to us right away; He makes us wait. There is purpose in your season of waiting. I have learned that during the times of waiting, God is preparing us for His promise. It is during our waiting that God teaches us things. Our character, faith, and ability are developed so that we can be and do all that He has called us to.

God takes us through a process… Will you trust it? Will you trust the process when it seems like the promise will never be fulfilled? Will you trust the process when things do not work out the way you think they should? Will you trust the process during the dark, scary, or painful moments? Will you trust the process?

DETOURS AND DELAYS

In the Book of Exodus, we find the children of Israel living as slaves in Egypt. They had a promise that God would deliver them and give them the promised land. After hundreds of years in slavery, God raises up a man named Moses as their deliverer. In chapter thirteen we see that Pharaoh, the king of Egypt, has finally agreed to let the Israelite people go free.

In Exodus 13:17-18 we read, *"When Pharaoh finally let the people go, God did not lead them along the main road that runs through Philistine territory, even though that was the shortest route to the Promised Land. God said, "If the people are faced with a battle, they might change their minds and return to Egypt." So,* **God led them in a roundabout way** *through the wilderness toward the Red Sea. Thus, the Israelites left Egypt like an army ready for battle"* (NLT). What we learn from this part of the story is that God does not always use the quickest path to get us where we are going. Sometimes God will lead us in a roundabout way to our promise, and yes, even through the wilderness. It is easy for us to look at the detour or the delay and become discouraged, disgruntled, or resentful. We need to trust God and His process, knowing that He always knows what is best and has our best interest in mind.

God knew that if He would have led the Israelite people down the quickest path, they would have had to face the Philistine army and go into battle. The battle would have scared and discouraged them more than the detour. It would have caused them to run back to Egypt and back into slavery.

God knows what is ahead of you, long before you ever get there. He knows what awaits you on the path ahead. Trust that if God has you in a moment of delay or if He has you taking a detour, He is doing it for your good. Do not get disgruntled by the detour. Do not become discouraged by the delay. Trust God! Trust the process!

Delay is not denial.

THE PROCESS BRINGS THE PROMISE

God came to the Prophet Samuel in First Samuel chapter sixteen and said, *"I have rejected Saul as king. Go to the tribe of Jesse where I have chosen one of his sons to be king."* Anointing someone to be king while Saul was still on the throne might not go well, and Samuel knew that. Samuel responded to God and told Him that he would be killed if Saul found out. So, God says, *"Take a cow and put together a sacrifice to Me and invite Jesse and his sons to the sacrifice."* When Samuel arrived in Bethlehem to speak with Jesse, the elders in the town were afraid. They were afraid because in those days when a prophet appeared it meant there was trouble. Samuel told them, "Do not worry. I have come to make a sacrifice to God, and you are invited." So, Jesse, his sons, and the whole town showed up to watch the sacrifice. As Jesse's sons arrived, Samuel had a hunch about who God wanted for the new king - Eliab, the oldest son. We read in 1 Samuel 16:6, *"When they arrived, Samuel took one look at Eliab and thought, "Surely this is the Lord's anointed!""* (NLT).

I am sure that Samuel had his own reasons for assuming that Eliab was who God had planned for the throne. After all, Eliab was the oldest and would have been first in line to receive his father's inheritance. Eliab was probably the tallest and most physically fit out of all his brothers. We read in 1 Samuel 16:7, *"But the Lord said to Samuel, "Don't judge by his appearance or height, for I have rejected him. The Lord does not see things the way you see them. People judge by outward appearance, but the Lord looks at the heart""* (NLT). So, one after the other, each of Jesse's sons passed in front of Samuel. How about this one? No. This one? Not him. This one? Not him either. Seven of Jesse's sons passed in front of Samuel. Finally, Samuel asked Jesse, *"Are there anymore?"* 1 Samuel 16:11b-12 states, *""There is still the youngest." Jesse replied. "But he's out in the fields watching the sheep and goats." "Send for him at once." Samuel said. "We will not sit down to eat until he arrives." So, Jesse sent for him. He was dark and handsome, with beautiful eyes. And the Lord said, "This is the one; anoint him"* (NLT).

So, Samuel anoints David, and then the story stops. There is a break in the story. When this part of the story ends, the Bible tells us that David went back to what he was doing before - watching the sheep and goats.

When I read this, I thought, "That doesn't make any sense. Why would God anoint David as king and then send him back to where He had him before (watching sheep and goats)? What was the point? God could have waited to anoint David until He was ready to make David king." God anointed David so far in advance because God wanted to take David through a process, and the anointing was a reminder of the promise that the process would bring.

A process is a series of actions or steps taken to achieve a particular end or goal. Some things needed to happen in David's life before he could be king. The same goes for you and me. There are some things that need to happen in our lives before we can step into what God has for us. A great example of process is the Chinese Bamboo Tree. The tree starts as a nut planted in the soil. It must be watered and fertilized every single day for five years before it finally breaks through the ground. If the watering or fertilizing process stops, the Chinese Bamboo Tree will die in the ground. During those five years that the nut is watered and fertilized, it spreads out its roots. In the fifth year, the Chinese Bamboo Tree finally breaks through the ground and grows to nearly ninety feet tall in just six weeks. The tree must take five long years of developing a strong, deep, and wide root system so it does not topple over when it is grown. We get frustrated when we do not get five-year results immediately. It is in the process that your root system is developed. This root system will give you nutrients when times get hard. This root system will give you strength when the winds of life blow. This root system will give you the stability you need to grow and go higher. The process is essential, and everyone must go through the process to get the results. Will you allow the waiting to develop you and make you better, or will you allow it to make you bitter? Let me encourage you… get better not bitter! You may say, "I'm not bitter." Your attitude, however, may say something different.

David could have quickly become bitter in his waiting, but he didn't. David knew that God was using the process to bring about His promise for him to be king. Bitterness is unbelief in the promises of God. If God says that the throne is yours, and that the kingdom is yours, then it is yours! It simply may not be time yet. Do not delay the fulfillment of your promise with bitterness. That's right, if you are bitter, you cannot receive all that God has for you. Moses declared in Numbers 23:19, *"God is not a man, so He does not lie! He is not human, so He does not change His mind. Has He ever spoken and failed to act? Has He ever promised and not carried it through?"* (NLT). People say, "I had faith, and God didn't do it." They are frustrated because they thought God said it would happen and it didn't. This is not how faith works. You cannot have faith in one moment and then faith leaves when you don't get what you want when you want it. Faith is what keeps you going until you see God do what He has promised. 2 Corinthians 5:7 declares, *"For we live by believing and not by seeing"* (NLT). The best way to lean into believing and trusting is by releasing control and expectations. Just believe with no strings attached.

ANOINTED, NOT APPOINTED

One thing that hinders a lot of people in trying to trust the process is that they mistake the anointing of God for the appointing of God. David had the anointing to be king, but he did not have the appointment to be king yet. Sometimes, you can have an anointing on your life to do something, but not the appointing. You may be anointed, but not yet appointed.

David could see the anointing. Other people could see the anointing. When Samuel poured the oil over David's head and anointed him as king, everyone was watching. You can see the anointing on your life. For example: you are a better salesperson than everyone else at work, you are a great singer, you have influence, you can counsel, you can lead, you can teach the Bible, etc. Other people can see it, too. They tell you how talented you are, how great you are, how anointed you are, and how far you will go. This then causes you to think, "I can see it. Others can see it. Why can't God see it? What is God waiting for?" We begin to think that it is our time to be more and do more. We become unsatisfied and discontented with where we are. We begin having tunnel vision.

What is tunnel vision? Tunnel vision happens when we are so focused on the light at the end of the tunnel that we cannot see what is happening around us, in us, and for us. Our eyes cannot adjust to our surroundings because all we can see is the light up ahead, the end goal, the destination. So, we miss things. We miss important information that can help us when we get out of the tunnel. We find ourselves tripping over things that are there to teach us something all because we cannot see. Do not become so focused on the destination that you neglect the journey. Do not become so focused on the promise that you neglect the process. It is the journey (process) that prepares you for success in the destination (promise).

PREPARATION IS KEY

After he was anointed, David's appointment was to watch the sheep and goats. Sometimes, we think that watching is just something we do to pass the time until we can do what we are "supposed to do." This is not true! If you are watching the sheep and goats right now, you are supposed to watch the sheep and goats. That is your appointment. There are lessons to be learned while sitting in the field watching the sheep and goats. The field teaches you lessons that prepare you for the palace. It teaches you how to appreciate the palace and to remain humble on the throne. Preparation must come before the opportunity. Although it looks as if nothing has changed, God is building your trust in Him, your character, your willingness to serve, and He is growing your giftings. Sit in that, appreciate it, and be content. It is for your good because without preparation, you will mess up the opportunity.

You can trust the process. God is preparing you for the opportunity that will come. This is what we see in David's life. David goes back to tend the sheep and what happens? 1 Samuel 16:14-19 states, *"Now the Spirit of the Lord had left Saul, and the Lord sent a tormenting spirit that filled him with depression and fear. Some of Saul's servants said to him, 'A tormenting spirit from God is troubling you. Let us find a good musician to play the harp whenever the tormenting spirit troubles you. He will play soothing music, and you will soon be well again.' "All right," Saul said. "Find me someone who plays well and bring him here." One of the servants said to Saul, "One of Jesse's sons from Bethlehem is a talented harp player. Not only that—he is a brave warrior, a man of war, and has good judgment. He is also a fine-looking young man, and the Lord is with him." So, Saul sent messengers to Jesse to say, "Send me your son David, the shepherd"'* (NLT). It was while David was tending the sheep and goats that he developed his ability to play the lyre and write music. This was an ability that was necessary for the opportunity! What would've been the result if all David did while he sat in the field was wonder why he was not yet king? What would have been the result if David sat in the field and complained about where he was rather than working on his music skills? The result would have been that his opportunity was delayed or that it was canceled altogether.

Now, let us fast forward to the story of David and Goliath in First Samuel chapter seventeen. 1 Samuel 17:32-36 states, *""Don't worry about this Philistine," David told Saul. "I'll go fight him!" "Don't be ridiculous!" Saul replied. "There's no way you can fight this Philistine and possibly win! You're only a boy, and he's been a man of war since his youth." But David persisted. "I have been taking care of my father's sheep and goats," he said. "When a lion or a bear comes to steal a lamb from the flock, I go after it with a club and rescue the lamb from its mouth. If the animal turns on me, I catch it by the jaw and club it to death. I have done this to both lions and bears, and I'll do it to this pagan Philistine, too, for he has defied the armies of the living God!"* (NLT). Again, the preparation had to come before the opportunity. It was in the field watching sheep and goats that David gained the experience of destroying a lion and a bear with his bare hands. Without the experience he gained in the field he would have never had the confidence he needed to go before Goliath. He would have never had the confidence to speak up and seize his moment!

David had to prepare. If he had never mastered the lyre, he never would have been chosen to play for Saul, and Saul would not have been familiar with him. If he had never killed the lion and the bear: Saul would not have let him face Goliath, David may not have had the confidence he needed to face Goliath, and the Israelites would not have accepted David as king. If David did not prepare, he would have squandered the opportunity. David, however, did prepare, and it led him to being appointed as king. Your preparation is leading you to the promise!

You may be in a season of waiting. Abraham waited twenty-five years. Joseph waited thirteen years. Moses waited forty years. Jesus waited thirty years. If God has you sitting in the waiting room, you are in good company. Maybe you have been waiting for a long time, and you are starting to wonder if God will ever do what He promised. Trust the process. Let your

YOUR PREPARATION IS LEADING YOU TO THE PROMISE!

faith be strengthened. Know that God is preparing you today for what He wants to do through you in the future. He is teaching you to trust Him, to be bold in your faith, He is growing your character, and He is fine-tuning your gifts. Trust Him – the process is bringing about the promise!

YOUR PROGRESS IS IN THE PROCESS

We must trust and go through the process to progress forward towards peace and healing. We must have the discipline to do the work that is required to create the thing that we say we want. Do you want the throne? Do you want the kingdom? Do you want the promise? You must have the discipline to go through what is required to be prepared for all that God has for you and has called or created you to be. We cannot give up halfway through the process. We must be willing to go all the way, even when it gets uncomfortable.

You will not be blessed for what you start. You will be blessed for what you complete.

In 2 Corinthians 8:10-12 the Apostle Paul states, *"Here is my advice: It would be good for you to finish what you started a year ago. Last year you were the first who wanted to give, and you were the first to begin doing it. Now you should finish what you started. Let the eagerness you showed in the beginning be matched now by your giving. Give in proportion to what you have. Whatever you give is acceptable if you give it eagerly. And give according to what you have, not what you don't have"* (NLT). It is good for us to finish the work or the process that we start. When it gets uncomfortable or hard, it is important for the time, energy, focus, openness, willingness, etc. that we are giving towards the process to match the eagerness we had at the beginning of the process. We need to be sure to give in proportion to what we have. What this means is if all you have to give towards the process is a little time, a little trust, or a little faith give that and give it well with eagerness. So, what does it take to trust the process?

- **See yourself as God sees you.** You are His and you have been bought with a price. Ephesians 2:10 says, *"For we are His workmanship, created in Christ Jesus for good works, which God prepared beforehand that we should walk in them"* (NKJV). God sees us as people of destiny and purpose. He prepared the work that we need to do to fulfill that destiny and purpose.

- **Be yourself.** Be real and authentic. Not who you feel everyone expects you to be or wants you to be, but be the bold and beautiful you that God created. We read in 1 Samuel 16:7, *"The Lord doesn't see things the way you see them. People judge by outward appearance, but the Lord looks at the heart"* (NLT). Many of us wear a mask. Let who you are on the inside be who you are on the outside.

- **Know yourself.** Know your strengths. Know your weaknesses. Lamentations 3:40 says, *"...let us test and examine our ways..."* (NLT). Become self-aware. This requires constant testing and examining of our minds, heart, intentions, behaviors, motives, etc.

- **Accept yourself.** You do not have to be perfect. Perfection is not all it's cracked up to be. We read in Psalm 139:14, *"...I am fearfully and wonderfully made; Marvelous are Your works, and that my soul knows very well"* (NKJV). You are God's masterpiece. It is important to understand that bad behavior does not make you a bad person. When you can learn to accept that you are God's workmanship, but have bad behaviors, mindsets, attitudes, etc. you can then move forward towards deliverance and healing.

- **Honor yourself.** Do what brings you joy and peace. If it robs you of your joy or peace, it is not worth your time. Honor yourself enough to not lie to yourself. Tell the truth. Tell the truth of who you are. Tell the truth about your feelings, motives, and intentions. Tell the truth about your bad behaviors and habits.

The process is necessary to go forward and to grow. Let's look at what the process is for doing the work required to achieve real change in our lives, relationships, mindsets, behaviors, and circumstances.

1. PAUSE AND BREATHE

Give yourself a break! It is unkind, unloving, and unrealistic to ask yourself to do something that you do not know how to do. Too often, we tell ourselves, "I should be here, or I should be there. I should be doing this or that." Give yourself a break if you don't know how to get where you want to go. Give yourself a break if you don't know how to deal with the problems you are facing. Give yourself a break if you don't know why you are feeling what you are feeling. Give yourself a break. Put a comma where you are, pause, and just breathe. When you doubt, pause. When you are angry, pause. When you are tired, pause. When you are stressed or frustrated, pause. When you are sad or hopeless, pause. And when you pause, **BREATHE!** Use the information you have to simply do better than you did yesterday. Stop beating yourself up for what you did not do or should be doing. Thank God for what He has brought you from and what He has brought you through. Pause, take a deep breath, and praise God for what He has done. Let it be a reminder to you that if God did it before, He will do it again! Then, go forward.

2. TELL THE TRUTH

We read in Proverbs 12:22, "*The Lord detests lying lips, but He delights in those who tell the truth*" (NLT). People have a habit of inventing fictions they will believe so they can ignore the truth they cannot accept. We must start being honest about our thoughts, our feelings, and our behaviors. We don't tell the truth about these things because we're afraid that we will be wrong, and we don't like to be wrong. Why do we not like to be wrong? Because being wrong hurts our egos. Do you really know what motivates you? Before you start doing the work, identifying the problems, and admitting the truth you must ask yourself, what are my intentions and what are my motives? You must know what you are wanting to cultivate your life into. You must have an idea of where you want to be and who you want to be when the work is finished.

Identifying your intentions and motives is crucial because working on yourself is going to be exhausting. It will be emotional, tense, and full of pressure. It's not easy. We are told in 2 Corinthians 13:5a to, "*Examine yourselves to see if your faith is genuine. Test yourselves...*" (NLT). If your intentions and motives are clear, you will be encouraged and empowered to stand against the repelling force of resistance.

Do you know what it is that makes you respond the way you do to certain situations? Is it something that happened to you in your childhood? Is it something that happened in a previous marriage? What makes you behave the way you do when you are hurt or when you are angry? When answering these questions, you must tell the whole truth. No excuses.

3. HAVE THE HARD CONVERSATIONS

A hard conversation is what many people would call confrontational. It is a conversation where you challenge or question. It is a conversation where you present or talk about a sensitive topic. Some call it "**CON-frontational**", but I have heard it called, "**CARE-frontational**". You have the hard conversations because you care enough about yourself or your relationship with someone to make things better. You have the hard conversation to clear things up, to get accurate information, or to establish a boundary. A hard conversation is just as hard to speak as it is to hear. A hard conversation challenges a behavior or something that you have been tolerating, accommodating, and accepting. You have the hard conversation about something that is no longer working and needs to change. When you have the hard conversation, whether it be with yourself or someone else, you will get resistance, rebellion, and pushback. The intention of the hard conversation will determine the outcome. If your intention is healing, you will find healing. If the intention is freedom, you will find freedom. If your intention is to find the truth, you will find the truth.

You must have the hard conversations. If the breakdown is within yourself, you must have the hard conversation with yourself. If the breakdown is in a relationship, you must have the hard conversation with that person(s). It is not always pretty. It will not feel good, and it will not be easy. But it is necessary. If you are willing to listen and tell the truth, healing and breakthrough can happen. You must be willing to discuss where and how the breakdown happened and you must be willing to be wrong. You must be willing to be wrong about what you thought or how you felt or what you said. You must be willing to be wrong about what you heard or how you interpreted what the other person said. You must be willing to be wrong about what you did and how you reacted or responded. It doesn't always mean you are wrong, but you must be willing to see another person's perspective. If you want to be positive, healed, and whole, you must be willing to do the work. When it gets hard, don't run. Face it.

4. CHALLENGE IT AND CHANGE IT

Change is not easy. It takes effort. Your willingness to face your "thing" is what will empower you to make changes in your life. You cannot accomplish personal change by covering your inner struggles and problems with denial, shifting blame, or by making excuses. To achieve personal change, you must be committed, persistent, determined, and patient. Don't rush it. Take your time.

Change is an inside job. When you do the work, when you work on yourself, you not only produce change in your life, but you produce change down in the depths of your soul. The thought of change can stir up resistance within us. You may lose focus after a few days, or you may find yourself doubting your ability to produce the change that you are working for.

Change cannot be forced, coerced, or demanded. Change is a journey. With change, you cannot say, "Do this and this will happen." Change is uncertain which can produce fear and anxiety. Change requires you to have a vision and a strategic plan for your life. There are four steps you can take towards accomplishing positive change...

- **Be a visionary for your change.** You cannot accomplish anything if you don't know what it is you want to accomplish. Maybe you are wanting to get rid of negative thinking and start thinking more positively. Maybe you are wanting to manage your mouth better by complaining or speaking less negatively. Maybe you are wanting to become the master of your emotions. Whatever the change may be, having a vision will give you a focus. Write it down and read it every day. Habakkuk 2:2 tells us to, "*Write the vision; make it plain, so he may run who reads it*" (ESV).

- **Give yourself permission to change.** Tell yourself that it is ok to change, to be different. Where you have been and what is expected of you is not who you are. You shape who you want to be. The best way to make the changes you wish to see in your life, is to get connected with people who have what you need, people who possess the characteristics you wish to possess. What they have will rub off on you. Therefore, relationships are very important. Relationships shape your world. Lock arms with people who will support you in your journey to change. Proverbs 27:17 says, "*As iron sharpens iron, so a friend sharpens a friend.*" (NLT).

- **Start small!** When you are doing the work and making changes in your life, it is ok to start small. You do not have to do a complete renovation of your life overnight. It is a process. We read in Zechariah 4:10a, "*Do not despise these small beginnings, for the Lord rejoices to see the work begin...*" (NLT). Just start and be patient with the process. Watch what will unfold.

- **Press! Push! Pursue!** When the voice of negativity says, "NO! You can't!" You say, "YES! I can!" I encourage you to stand strong through the process! If all your hard work has not taken you where you want to go, work harder. If you fall, get back up. If you are tired, rest, and keep pushing. If your vision has not come to fruition, keep your focus. If you become discouraged, encourage yourself. If you grow insecure, believe in yourself and be confident in your ability to change. Never accept defeat in life; success is the only option for you! We read in Matthew 19:26, "*Jesus looked at them and said, "With man this is impossible, but with God all things are possible"* (ESV).

Change can create problems but fear not! Problems are our friends! We learn from our problems. Problems reveal what kind of change is required of us. Adversities and trials touch everyone's life; no one is exempt. Remember that diamonds are produced by pressure. Our trials come and produce positive change in our lives. I don't know what will happen in your change experience. What I do know is that something great and outstanding will be revealed in every area of your life!

Life is spelled like this, **C-H-A-N-G-E**. What is the point of calling a "thing" a "thing" if you are not willing to change? Change is a sign that you are alive and growing.

I know one thing to be true, this process we call "life" takes work. We must work on ourselves, work on our relationships, and work on our issues and choices. If we don't do the work, we will suffer and lack so much unnecessarily.

FIVE

INTERRUPT THE STORY

You will know the truth,
and the truth will make you free.
John 8:32 (ERV)

Everyone has a story. We all have a past, a present, and a future story. No matter how you define or describe it, your past story has somehow influenced or affected your present story in a positive or negative way. Your present story will influence your future story.

If life is not going in the direction that you want it to take; if your present story is not going where you want it to go… Interrupt the story! For example: when you make the decision to stop struggling, you'll stop. When you make the decision to live your life in happiness, forgiveness, and prosperity, you will. Simply give yourself the permission to be OKAY! Give yourself the permission to move forward in the fullness of peace, joy, and love.

You do not have to stay where you are. You might be thinking that where you are isn't so bad. You may think that where you are in life is good or even great. Know this truth… there is more and there is greater for you! You can live an "exceedingly, abundantly above life." What do I mean? Jesus said in John 10:10, "*I am come that they might have life, and that they might have it* **more abundantly**" (KJV). Jesus did not come just to give you any ole ordinary life. He came to give you a life that is rich, satisfying, full, and overflowing! If these words do not describe where you are, you are living beneath your privilege. Jesus paid the price for you to live a life filled with the fullness of God. Your story does not have to be a sad one. Your story does not have to be a story of brokenness, pain, bitterness, fear, loss, or defeat. With God's help, you can live higher and better. You can walk in the greater and grander! Stop living beneath your privilege. Stop retelling the sad story, the defeated story, the bitter and broken story. Interrupt the story!

3 LIES YOU MUST IGNORE

Life, people, circumstance, self, and the devil will all tell you lies to keep you where you are, to keep your story a negative one, and to keep you from moving forward to a better place. To interrupt the story, you must ignore the lies. Here are three lies to ignore...

LIE #1: You are not strong enough to do this. Do not undervalue and underestimate yourself. You are powerful. The same power that raised Jesus from the dead lives within you. The Apostle Paul tells us in Romans 8:11, "*The Spirit of God, who raised Jesus from the dead, lives in you*" (NLT). So don't believe the lie that says you won't make it and you don't have it in you to succeed. The Spirit of God is in you, empowering you through it all. If there is ever a time that you are weak, you can take confidence in knowing that God is for you, and He has your back. The Psalmist said, "*God is our refuge and strength, always ready to help in times of trouble*" (Psalm 46:1 NLT). When you have reached the end of your rope, God is always ready to step in and help you. You're His kid and your story matters to Him.

LIE #2: You are not brave enough to do this. Keep your head up and your face forward. March on with the confidence that God is with you, and He is for you. Joshua 1:9 says, *"This is my command—be strong and courageous! Do not be afraid or discouraged. For the Lord your God is with you wherever you go"* (NLT). It is okay to be scared. Fear is a part of life. It is when fear controls us that we have a problem. Press through the fear. When you are scared but you still do it anyway, that is bravery and courage. 2 Timothy 1:7 declares, *"For God gave us a spirit not of fear but of power and love and self-control"* (ESV). Walk in the power God has given you, love every moment, and take control of your life.

LIE #3: You have messed up too much to have any hope now. Never disqualify yourself from something that God's grace has qualified you for. In 2 Corinthians 5:17b, The Apostle Paul declares, *"...Anyone who belongs to Christ has become a new person. The old life is gone; a new life has begun"* (NLT). Where you have been does not determine where you are going. God's grace is sufficient to cover your past mistakes, your bad behavior, and any slip ups. You have a hope for the future. God has a plan for your life, and nothing can nullify that. His purpose is eternal. God told the Prophet Jeremiah, *"'For I know the plans I have for you,' says the Lord. 'They are plans for good and not for disaster, to give you a future and a hope'"* (Jeremiah 29:11 NLT). Your story is never hopeless. God always has a good plan for your future. Trust that and let it be your anchor.

No matter what is happening on the outside, no matter what you are feeling on the inside, no matter what kind of lies you are hearing, God's voice is louder, His love is bigger, He is stronger, and His grace is all-sufficient!

SET BOUNDARIES

Boundaries are an essential part of interrupting and protecting the story or pattern in your life. If you have unhealthy work habits: a workaholic, constantly working. If there is no time for rest, fun, or family; you need to set a boundary. If you have unhealthy behaviors or patterns in a relationship such as: allowing someone to control or manipulate you, to abuse you mentally, emotionally, or physically, or you allow someone to cheat on you, talk down to you or disrespect you… You need to set a boundary.

Healthy boundaries are not walls to block others out. They are barriers to set us free to love the right people, including ourselves.

We tend to forget or even ignore the importance of boundaries. Too often, we don't establish them. In other situations, we ignore them or deny them. When a boundary is violated, it can lead to a breakdown in a relationship or even in your physical, spiritual, emotional, or mental health. Honoring and maintaining your boundaries is a statement and demonstration of personal and mutual respect. A boundary is a structure, expectation, request, or system that you put in place to define, prescribe, limit, or exclude a behavior, people, or experiences that are not in alignment with who you are, who you want to be, or where you are trying to go in life. Boundaries are useful safety measures. They keep us focused and on course. Boundaries keep us aware of how far we can go and how much we can do. Boundaries make others aware of what we expect, accept, allow, accommodate, and tolerate in our lives.

Boundaries are not walls that keep other people out. They are parameters that keep you safe! Boundaries are a way to communicate to others that you have self-respect, self-worth, and standards for your life. When you do not have clear boundaries or your boundaries are not honored, you can easily be manipulated, used, or violated by others. Be clear about your boundaries. What do you need? Is it less stress and more peace? Then set the appropriate boundaries to eliminate stress and have peace around you. Maybe you are so stressed because you bring your work home with you every night. Evaluate your situation. When you are at work, are you socializing or are you working? Draw boundaries. Prioritize getting the work done before socializing with others. Maybe you are taking on too many projects at work. Maybe you are saying, "yes" instead of exercising your "no." Whatever your situation, evaluate and then begin drawing boundaries.

BOUNDARIES ARE YOUR RESPONSIBILITY. YOU DECIDE WHAT IS OR IS NOT ALLOWED IN YOUR LIFE.

___

After you are clear about what boundaries you need and after you define what your boundaries are, you need to announce your boundaries. Here is where many fail. Many people recognize that they need a boundary, but they never announce and establish it. When someone crosses a boundary or when you feel dishonored or disrespected, announce your boundary.

Here is how you announce your boundary. Inform others about your boundary and then inform them when they have violated it. For example: when you find yourself in a disagreement and someone takes it too far and starts calling you names, respond with, "I hear what you are saying, and I want you to know that it is no longer acceptable for you to call me anything other than my name."

Once you have drawn and announced your boundary, you need to identify the parameters of your boundary. Meaning, you need to identify how the boundary will operate or how you will operate within that boundary. For example: "I know you probably did not mean to be disrespectful, but I have decided that in order for me to be and feel respected, I cannot accommodate people calling me out of my name."

Once you have identified how the boundary works for you, educate others on how the new boundary operates in your life. For example: "Here is my request. When you are talking to me, I am asking you to refrain from calling me anything other than my name." It is imperative to communicate the consequences of violating your boundaries. When you have a clear boundary, you must have a clear consequence for when it is violated. A boundary without a violation consequence is an empty threat. Be clear about what will happen when the boundary is violated. For example: "If you insist on calling me names when we are talking, I will remove myself from the conversation." You don't have to get upset and start acting ridiculous. Announce the boundary and the consequence for violating the boundary and then stick to it. If the boundary is crossed, walk away. You may have to be flexible at first. If name calling has been something you have tolerated in a relationship, it may take some time for the bad behavior to be corrected and for a new behavior to form.

Be sure to remind others of the boundary when it is crossed and if they continue to cross it, walk away. For example: "Remember, I have asked you not to swear at me or not to call me anything other than my name or not to yell at me, etc. If you continue, I will remove myself from the conversation." If they continue simply say, "Until you are ready to honor my request, I'm leaving." Then walk away. Do not stay and continue to allow others to disrespect you or violate your boundaries. When you draw a line in the sand, if they cross the line, don't back up and draw another line. When the line is crossed, show them that the consequence is in place. Having a boundary is learning to say, "no". Exercise your "no".

You do not have to diminish yourself to please anyone. Have boundaries. Honor your boundaries.

Boundaries are your responsibility. It is not up to anyone other than you to decide what works for you. You decide what is or is not allowed in your life. Draw boundaries and enforce them. Pay attention to who has issues with the boundaries you draw. These are usually people who are intentionally or unintentionally trying to control or manipulate you. I've learned that the only people who get upset about you setting boundaries are the ones benefitting from you not having any. Don't back down. You have the right to set the standard for your life. If they are not okay with the standard you have set for your life, let them walk away. You are allowed to set boundaries for your life, and you are allowed to say goodbye to anyone who does not respect them. So set healthy boundaries for your life and interrupt the pattern or story that you want to change!

YOU MATTER

Do not feel guilty for doing what is best for you. You matter. Who you are matters. What you do matters. How you do what you do matters. When you don't know that you matter, you will take on somebody else's crazy and make it about you. You have your own stuff to process. For example: a child with a "mean" relative will make that person's meanness all about them. The child will begin to think the person is mean because of something they have done or did not do. The child will begin to think the person is mean because of who they are. Truthfully, the difficult relative has a story. Something in their past causes them to behave badly. Something in their story has taught them that their meanness is necessary, that being spiteful is necessary. We all have a story. We get our meaning and our mattering from our story. When you come to the realization that you matter you will find the empowerment you need to interrupt the story.

It begins with having a strong "no". So many people suffer from having weak and flabby "no" muscles. I used to be one of those people. I said "yes" to everything. I always said "yes" because I was afraid if I said "no" people wouldn't like me or even love me. My validation and sense of acceptance and accomplishment came from pleasing others with my "yes" even if it was at the expense of myself, my peace, my rest, my comfort, or my joy. You must have a solid, strong "no" muscle that you can stand in. You also must have a strong "yes" muscle. You must be able to say "no" to the things that do not honor you, bring you joy, or bring you peace. And you don't have to explain your "no". You matter and your "no" matters. Don't ever back up on your "no". Do not draw your line in the sand and then when someone crosses it, back up and draw another line. "No" means "no". Stand on your line and stand in your "no". You also need to stand for your "yes". When you matter, you stand **IN** your "no" and **FOR** your "yes". Interrupt the story and the pattern in your life by letting "no" mean "no" and "yes" mean "yes". You choose what is or is not allowed or acceptable in your life.

You matter and what you think matters. If you don't manage your mind, it's not going to produce positive results for you. If you can't win in your own mind, what do you think you are going to do out in this crazy world? If you do not keep your thinking in order, your thought life will drive you crazy and over a cliff. Simplify your thinking. For example: do not over complicate things in your own mind by trying to figure out what someone else is going to say in response to what you plan to say. You matter! If what you want to say is "no" or "yes". Just say it. If what you want to say sets a boundary, exposes a lie, or tells the truth, just say it. Stand in it and stand for it… because **YOU MATTER!** Get a grip on your thoughts. Stop thinking about what "they" said or did. Stop rehearsing that argument or disagreement in your mind. Stop letting people live rent free in your head. Stop thinking about what might happen. Stop worrying about what could be. If your thoughts do not bring you peace, stop thinking them. You can either have control of your mind or your mind will control you.

You matter. What you want matters and what you feel matters. You must unlearn the lessons that the adults from your childhood taught you. Maybe the lesson you learned was that what you know, want, or feel does not matter. So now, you find yourself comparing yourself to other people. This is an act of violence against yourself when you compare yourself to other people. Interrupt the story with a "no" to what you do not want and with a "yes" to what you want to attract, create, allow, and bring into your life.

You matter. How you show up matters. Every moment of every day, no matter where you are, what you are doing, or who you are with… **YOU MATTER!** You are demonstrating the power, the love, and the Spirit of God in everything that you do and everywhere you go. So, how you show up in a room looking and acting, it matters! Stop showing up broken, depressed, bitter, angry, and resentful. Stop showing up worried, anxious, and afraid. Stop showing up tired and pitiful. Stop showing up looking like the victim and defeated. Stop showing up looking like what you've been through. It does not matter who raised you or how they raised you; you matter. It does not matter what "they" did or said or how "they" treated you; you matter. It does not matter that you are not exactly where you would like to be in life; you matter! When you understand that regardless, you matter, you are not phased or bothered by the past, by people, or by circumstances.

When you begin repeatedly telling yourself that sad ole story, stop it because you matter. If somebody had the privilege and the honor of walking into your life and enjoying relationship with you, and they did not have the good sense to stay, you need to be glad to be rid of them! You matter!

Stop chasing things that are beneath the truth of who you are…
- **You are a child of God…**
  "But to all who believed Him and accepted Him, He gave the right to become children of God." (John 1:12, NTL).

- **You are a friend of God…**
  "I no longer call you slaves because a master doesn't confide in his slaves. Now you are My friends, since I have told you everything the Father told me." (John 15:15, NLT).

- **You are justified and at peace with God...**
  "Therefore, since we have been made right in God's sight by faith, we have peace with God because of what Jesus Christ our Lord has done for us." (Romans 5:1, NLT).

- **You are a temple of God...**
  "Don't you realize that all of you together are the temple of God and that the Spirit of God lives in you?" (1 Corinthians 3:16, NLT).

- **You are God's possession...**
  "For God bought you with a high price. So, you must honor God with your body." (1 Corinthians 6:20, NLT).

- **You are an heir of God...**
  "Now you are no longer a slave but God's own child. And since you are His child, God has made you, His heir." (Galatians 4:7, NLT).

- **You are a new person...**
  "This means that anyone who belongs to Christ has become a new person. The old life is gone; a new life has begun!" (2 Corinthians 5:17, NLT).

- **You are free...**
  "So Christ has truly set us free. Now make sure that you stay free, and don't get tied up again..." (Galatians 5:1, NLT).

- **You are chosen and holy...**
  "Even before He made the world, God loved us and chose us in Christ to be holy and without fault in His eyes." (Ephesians 1:4, NLT).

- **You are God's masterpiece created for good works...**
  "For we are God's masterpiece. He has created us anew in Christ Jesus, so we can do the good things He planned for us long ago." (Ephesians 2:10, NLT).

Stop holding on to mindsets, behaviors, ways of living and being, habits, things, and people that weigh you down. You matter! Stop behaving in ways that do not honor who God has called and created you to be. You matter! What you do matters. How you do it matters. Moment by moment you must remind yourself, "How I am showing up in this moment, how I am standing in this moment, how I am speaking in this moment, how I am sharing who I am and Whose I am in this moment, how I am being and acting in this moment, it matters because I matter!"

In case you haven't been told… **YOU MATTER!**

CALL A THING A THING

SIX

IT AIN'T WORKIN'

...Jesus has been given a ministry that is far superior to the old priesthood, for He is the one who mediates for us a far better covenant with God, based on better promises. If the first covenant had been faultless, there would have been no need for a second covenant to replace it.
Hebrews 8:6-7 (NLT)

We are all guilty of holding on to things, people, past seasons, offences, mindsets, habits, behaviors, and other things that we need to let go of. We hold on to them because they are comfortable and familiar. For some, these ways of living and being are all a person knows. For others, letting go is uncomfortable and even scary. We give little regard to the fact that these things do not serve us in a positive way. In fact, we ignore that they harm us, not help us. We ignore the fact that we are doing ourselves a disservice by holding on to them.

In Hebrews 8:6-7 we read, *"But now Jesus, our High Priest, has been given a ministry that is far superior to the old priesthood, for He is the one who mediates for us a far better covenant with God, based on better promises. If the first covenant had been faultless, there would have been no need for a second covenant to replace it.* " (NLT) These people in Hebrews chapter eight were holding on to the old covenant instead of embracing the new covenant. They were holding on to something that was inferior, something that had become less than God's best. They were holding on to traditions, mindsets, and ways of living that were not working for them. This sounds familiar. We hold on to our way of doing things. We hold on to our preferences. We hold on to our ways of doing things. We hold on to our pain, attitudes, mindsets, behaviors, and habits. We hold tightly to our offences and grudges. We keep a firm grip on our past seasons. We keep running back to unhealthy relationships.

Let me serve you notice today… THEY AIN'T WORKIN'!

Holding on to the pain ain't workin'!
Being angry ain't workin'!
Being mean and nasty ain't workin'!
Holding that grudge ain't workin'!
Conforming to the culture ain't workin'!
Continuing to behave badly ain't workin'!
Being stuck in your past ain't workin'!
Running back to those unhealthy relationships ain't workin'!
That habit ain't workin'!
That negative, defeated, pitiful mindset ain't workin'!
Being afraid, worrying, and doubting ain't workin'!
That thing you're addicted to ain't workin'!
Pride ain't workin'!
That bad attitude ain't workin'!
Being insecure ain't workin'!
Continuing to look back instead of looking forward ain't workin'!
Doing life how you have been doing it ain't workin'!

Holding on to these things does not make us better, it make us bitter. You think you're holding on to them, but the truth is, they are holding on to you. They hold you back, stunt your growth, crush your spirit, disable your mobility, kill your passion, and make you look ugly. I don't know about you, but I don't want anything that is going to make me look ugly.

CONFRONT THE KINGS

I'm not a fighter. I don't like to fight; however, I will fight if you mess with the wrong thing. The Book of Joshua is for fighters. In the Book of Joshua, we find God moving Israel into the promised land – the land He said belonged to them. The thing is, they were only going to possess that promise if they fought for it. That's right, they had to fight for it. The same applies to you and me. God has promises for all of us, but we must possess them by fighting for them.

pos·sess: |pə'zes| - *verb*
to seize and take control of; to take into one's possession; to enter and control firmly

Taking possession of what God has promised is a process and usually involves a fight. There is always a purpose behind your fight. The greater the fight, the greater the promise. If you are going to let go of and conquer that which is not working in and for your life, you are going to have to fight.

The promise is yours. That means it is yours to fight for, take dominion of, and possess. This means that staying in your comfort zone is not an option. You must be willing to get uncomfortable and do the uncomfortable. When attempting to possess your promise, you do not have time to be concerned with comfort. Even though you may be grateful and thankful for where you are in life right now, you must understand that it is going to require more for you to get to where you are trying to go. You may have to confront some things. You may have to confront some of your own traditions to get what God has for you. You might have to break some bad habits. You might have to let go of some people. You might have to step out of your culture. Your culture may be calling you to think, act, or live one way but your hunger and thirst for something greater and grander is calling you another way. You may have to unlearn something that you were taught as a child – mindsets, attitudes, behaviors, or ways of being and doing things. Do not be surprised if God and the promise He has for you requires you to learn a new culture, get a new perspective, or have a new way of thinking.

**THERE IS
A PURPOSE
BEHIND
YOUR FIGHT.**

**THE GREATER
THE FIGHT,
THE GREATER
THE PROMISE.**

God is calling you higher. He may be calling you to live differently. He is calling you to something greater. The problem is that it is not easy to step outside of habits, behaviors, mindsets, or cultures. Yes, there are external forces that we must fight and get the victory over so that we can move forward into the greater destiny that God is calling us to. We will deal with those later. Most of the time the fight is with an internal force that we must get the victory over so that we can possess our promise. When we think about getting the victory, we think about getting the victory over someone else, a situation, or the devil. Getting victory over external forces is valid and necessary, but many times we need to get the victory over internal territory. We need to get the victory when the battle is raging on the inside of us.

We try to look cute. We try to look like we have it all together and have everything figured out. The truth is that everyone has something ugly up under all their cuteness. Everyone has issues they need to work through. You may look good, and you may smell good, but be not deceived, up under all that is a "thing" – a habit, behavior, pain, mindset, attitude, belief, pride, ego, fear, jealousy, insecurity, and the list goes on. Other people cannot see it because the fight is not external, it is internal. Not only is the fight on the inside, but the bleeding is on the inside, the pain is on the inside, the brokenness is on the inside. The exhaustion, the hopelessness, the struggle, and the wrestling is all happening on the inside. That is why someone who looks totally "normal" suddenly snaps and harms themselves or others.

As we look at this story about Joshua, we are going to see a story about an external fight, but I want you to see it from an internal point of view. In Joshua chapter ten, we find that Israel has gone into the land, fought, and won the battle. Joshua is so exhausted. He looks up and he prays, *"Let the sun stand still over Gibeon, and the moon over the valley of Aijalon"* (Joshua 10:12, NLT). God heard Joshua's prayer and the sun stood still. The sun stayed in the middle of the sky until Joshua and all of Israel won the victory over their enemies. Joshua realizes that he and Israel were not in the fight alone. God was fighting with them. Joshua says, *"There has never been a day like this one before or since, when the Lord answered such a prayer. Surely the Lord fought for Israel that day!"* (Joshua 10:14, NLT).

Look at what happens next, *"Then Joshua and the Israelite army returned to their camp at Gilgal. During the battle, the five kings escaped and hid in a cave at Makkedah."* (Joshua 10:15-16, NLT). Joshua and the Israelites fight these five armies but the kings of these five armies have hidden. Look at what Joshua does, *"When Joshua heard that they* (the kings) *had been found, he issued this command: "Cover the opening of the cave with large rocks, and place guards at the entrance to keep the kings inside. The rest of you continue chasing the enemy and cut them down from the rear. Don't give them a chance to get back to their towns, for the Lord your God has given you victory over them." So Joshua and the Israelite army continued the slaughter and completely crushed the enemy. They totally wiped out the five armies except for a tiny remnant that managed to reach their fortified towns. Then the Israelites returned safely to Joshua in the camp at Makkedah. After that, no one dared to speak even a word against Israel. Then Joshua said, "Remove the rocks covering the opening of the cave, and bring the five kings to me." So they brought the five kings out of the cave—the kings of Jerusalem, Hebron, Jarmuth, Lachish, and Eglon. When they brought them out, Joshua told the commanders of his army, "Come and put your feet on the kings' necks." And they did as they were told. "Don't ever be afraid or discouraged," Joshua told his men. "Be strong and courageous, for the Lord is going to do this to all of your enemies." Then Joshua killed each of the five kings and impaled them on five sharpened poles, where they hung until evening. As the sun was going down, Joshua gave instructions for the bodies of the kings to be taken down from the poles and thrown into the cave where they had been hiding. Then they covered the opening of the cave with a pile of large rocks, which remains to this very day"* (Joshua 10:17-27, NLT). What had become the hiding place for these five kings had now become their burial ground.

Joshua was a fighter. He had an instinct to fight. Every fight he engaged in, he won. Why? Because the hand of the Lord was on his life.

When the hand of God is on your life, the result is undeniable victory and success.

In our story we have a collision of five nations and their kings that have come together to fight Joshua and the Israelites. There would have been six, but because of how successful Israel was the Gibeonites chose to stand with them. Joshua had the other enemies on the run. The five kings were so scared that they ran and hid. What is funny about the whole thing is that these same kings were once pursuing Joshua. There comes a time in the fight when God turns the whole thing around, and what used to have its foot on you, you now have your foot on it.

The five kings are hiding because they are losing the battle. All of this was happening in Makkedah. It was significant that it happened in Makkedah. Makkedah represented the promise land. The enemy is standing in the middle of the promise, and it belongs to Joshua and the Israelites. The problem is that they lost it all because previous generations had fled the land and when they left, other people moved in and they inhabited what the previous generations ran away from. What we learn from this is that any time you flee or run away from a battle, you leave room for someone else to come in and take over. If we look at it from that perspective, in essence, these five kings and their armies are squatters. A squatter is someone who has no right to be in a place, but they have been there so long that they are determined that they are not going anywhere. These squatters had taken control and possession of what really belonged to the people of God. I wonder how many squatters are sitting on things that belong to you, but you don't have what it takes to uproot them and get them out.

You may have past hurts, brokenness, pain, bitterness, unforgiveness, anger, fear, anxiety, worry, etc. sitting on your peace and your joy. You may have negative mindsets, habits, behaviors, attitudes, pride, etc. sitting on your blessed and balanced future. Maybe these things are sitting on your family, your finances, your career, your marriage, your friendships, etc. They have been sitting there so long that they're determined they aren't going anywhere. Do not let past hurts, pain, brokenness, and anger infect your current relationships or keep you from walking in peace and joy. Do not allow negative mindsets to hold you back in your career. Do not allow bad habits to ruin your finances. Do not allow bad behaviors, attitudes, or pride destroy your family, marriage, or other relationships. You must face these things, uproot them, and get them out. If you want what rightfully belongs to you; you are in for a fight! Matthew 11:12 declares, *"...the kingdom of heaven suffers violence, and the violent take it by force"* (NKJV). So, fight for it! Take it by force!

The five kings and their armies were squatters, and they were sitting on what belonged to God's people. Joshua had fought all the external forces. Now it was time to fight all the internal forces that were sitting on the promise. Those kings that went into hiding had to be dealt with. When they found them, Joshua's men asked him what he wanted them to do with the kings. He tells them to roll a stone in front of the cave because he still had some fighting to do. There are times that you must roll a stone in front of things that you have not yet conquered.

What do I mean? You have not conquered it completely, but you have it under control. You have not conquered it yet, but you know what it is, you see it for what it is, you know where it is, you know where it came from, you can call it by its name, and you have it under control. You cannot let it mess up your momentum. You must go after what you need to go after. For example: You may struggle with insecurities, but it is not holding you back in your career or your relationships. You may struggle with fear, but it is not keeping you from going for greater. You may have some anger issues, but you are not erupting at the smallest difficulty. You know you need to confront these things. You know they must go, but you have them under control while you confront some other issues. For example: imagine that you walk into a room in your home, and you see a stain with a bubble in your ceiling. You call someone to fix what was broken. You then realize that you must call someone else because even though it was stained and broken in that spot, even though the problem was in that spot, the actual source of that issue was in an entirely different location in the roof. So, the spot in the ceiling was not where the problem originated but was a warning sign. It was a red flag. Don't ever ignore the warning signs because the result is you having to deal with a bigger issue. It showed up in one place, but it came from somewhere else. Let me put it like this... You lose your temper with someone in one situation, but the reason you did it is because of something else that happened in an entirely different situation. Instead of dealing with the problem you are having on your job, you hold it in, come home, and then take it out on everyone in your house. A teacher knows that if a child acts up in the classroom, the real problem is usually initiated at home. You're mean and rude to someone and it isn't because you are a mean and rude person or because you don't like that person. You are mean and rude because you're jealous of them or want what they have. Until you deal with that jealousy and learn to be happy with yourself and what you have, your behavior will never change.

Joshua is fighting these five different armies at the same time. He is fighting them because of these kings that are hiding in the cave. These kings are the people who built the armies. These kings gave them the weapons. These kings are the people who organized and strategized. So, Joshua is in one place having to fight these things that originated from somewhere else. Whatever your "thing" is, you must get to the root of it. You will never see new fruit until you deal with the root.

Joshua had the kings in a cave, and he was conquering everything that was in reach. You better get your kings under control. You better get the source of your "thing" under control so that you are free to conquer everything else that is in front of you. God is calling you higher. He is offering you something better. He is presenting you with something greater. Get your "thing" under control and **GO FOR IT!** Go for peace! Go for joy! Go for prosperity! Go for that dream! Go for the restoration in the relationship! Go for it all! Possess the promise! It belongs to you!

Even though Joshua was conquering everything in front of him, he could not stop there. He was conquering everything that stemmed from the five kings; however, he still needed to deal with the kings. It didn't matter how many foes he defeated. He couldn't really be called a champion, a winner, or a victor until he went back and confronted what was still living and hiding in the cave. If all you do is deal with the stain in the ceiling, and you never deal with the source of the problem, you are going to be painting over that stain for the rest of your life. The repair bill will be high, and it will be constant. You will spend your life trying to cover up what you will not correct. You will waste your life trying to cover up things you will not confront. Sooner or later, you must go back to the cave and confront the kings. You can kill the army, but if you do not kill the kings, the army will rise again.

Stop being in denial. You can demand excellence out of your children, but if you don't change the environment you're raising them in, they will never change. You may have carried your "thing" for months or even years. You must decide that time is up! It is unhealthy to not confront what needs to be confronted. It is unhealthy to not be able to verbalize what needs to be said. We all walk around confrontational. We talk a big game and say things like, "You don't want any of this! Don't mess with me!" We can confront everybody, but we never confront ourselves. We never confront our hatefulness, anger, bitterness, laziness, or judgmental spirit. We never confront that dominating spirit that shuts everybody down and they have to walk on eggshells around us. It is time to start confronting yourself. Stop blaming everybody else. Confront what needs to be confronted and correct what needs to be corrected so that you can recover what needs to be recovered. The key to your recovery is being willing to confront your kings.

Confront your "thing", because anything you cannot confront, you cannot conquer!

Joshua goes back to the cave, and he tells them to roll the stone away. It was time for him to confront what he needed to conquer. They brought the kings out. He calls his men over and he tells them to put their feet on the neck of the kings. Then they killed the kings. Put your "thing" under your foot and kill it because **IT AIN'T WORKIN'!** It is keeping you from your promise. It is keeping you from reaching greater. It is holding you back from reaching your fullest potential. There is more for you to possess. **GO FOR IT!**

PRESS. PUSH. PURSUE.

There is more to possess. There is more for you in this life. There is a better place than where you are right now in life. Even if you have no complaints about where you are… there is more! There is a new season waiting on you. God is saying, "Look at the land I have prepared for you! Go and possess it." He is willing to navigate us, but we must be willing to press, push, and pursue it! We cannot base the direction of our journey on how things look or appear to be. We do not walk by what we can see, we walk by our faith (2 Corinthians 5:7).

Stand strong! If all your hard work has not taken you where you want to go, work harder. If you fall, get back up. If you are tired, rest and then keep pushing. If your dream has not yet come true, keep pursuing it. If you become discouraged, encourage yourself. If you grow insecure, remind yourself who you are in Christ. Victory is the only outcome for you because the hand of the Lord is upon you!

I encourage you today that no matter what…
- **PRESS** toward the greater and higher God is calling you to.
- **PUSH** through doubt, fear, insecurity, negativity, and other opposing forces.
- **PURSUE** every promise God has for you.

SEVEN

KNOW YOUR ENEMY

...so that Satan will not outsmart us.
For we are familiar with his evil schemes.
2 Corinthians 2:11 (NLT)

According to Ephesians 6:12 we are all in a war, but do we really know who we're fighting? Do we know our enemy? Our enemy is not: our neighbor, a fellow church member, our co-worker, our spouse, our children, our siblings, or our friends. In Ephesians 6:12 the Apostle Paul states, *"For we are not fighting against flesh-and-blood enemies..."* (NLT). There are two forces at work in the world — **GOOD** and **EVIL**. God is good. Lucifer (Satan) is evil. Our real enemy is Satan. Satan and the forces of hell are who we are fighting and wrestling with. Since Satan cannot hurt God, he fights you and me – God's children. So, your fight is not against people or even circumstances. Your fight is against the devil.

Peter tells us to, *"Stay alert! Watch out for your great enemy, the devil. He prowls around* **like** *a roaring lion, looking for someone to devour"* (1 Peter 5:8, NLT). Your enemy is walking around seeking someone to devour! Here's the good news: that "someone" does not have to be you!

The enemy studies our every move. He observes our reactions and our words, and he uses them to his advantage. He discovers what upsets us. He finds out what breaks our heart or hurts us. He learns what pushes our buttons, and he figures out what tempts us to sin, think wrong thoughts, or behave badly. The enemy studies you and me, his opponents. He gets to know us. Yet, we don't study him or get to know him, his strategies, or how he works and operates. Any good sports team or army studies their opponent. We need to study ours.

We can learn the enemy's tactics through God's Word and avoid being deceived and trapped. We can be prepared to fight and win by getting to know our enemy!

THE ENEMY IS A LOSER BECAUSE GOD IS GREATER!

One thing you must know about your adversary is that he is a fake, a fraud, a counterfeit. According to 1 Peter 5:8, the enemy is **LIKE** a roaring lion. He is not actually a roaring lion. Jesus, however, is the actual Lion of the Tribe of Judah. What does this mean for you and me? It means that we are fighting **FROM** victory not **FOR** victory. The Apostle Paul wrote, "*...in all these things we are more than conquerors* **through Him** *that loved us*" (Romans 8:37, KJV). You already have the victory through Him that loved you enough to die for you. When Jesus died and rose again, He defeated everything you will ever face.

When facing our enemy, we must always remember that:

1. **Satan is a loser.** Colossians 2:15 tells us that Jesus, "*...disarmed the spiritual rulers and authorities. He shamed them publicly by His victory over them on the cross*" (NLT).

2. **Our God is greater.** We find this declaration in the scripture, "*For the Lord your God is the God of gods and Lord of lords. He is the great God, the mighty and awesome God...*" (Deuteronomy 10:17, NLT).

3. **We have victory.** The Apostle Paul declared, *"The God of peace will soon crush Satan under your feet..."* (Romans 16:20, NLT).

THE ENEMY HAS AN ASSIGNMENT AGAINST YOU

Jesus stated in John 10:10, *"The thief's purpose is to steal and kill and destroy..."* (NLT). We walk around and live our lives each day like there is not an enemy of our souls. We must always be on guard, watchful, and aware. The enemy is always planning ways to steal from us, plotting ways to kill every good thing in our lives, and looking for ways to destroy us. Paul addresses this and tells us how to approach Satan and his attacks. The Apostle Paul says in Ephesians 6:10-14, *"A final word: Be strong in the Lord and in His mighty power. Put on all of God's armor so that you will be able to stand firm against all strategies of the devil. For we are not fighting against flesh-and-blood enemies, but against evil rulers and authorities of the unseen world, against mighty powers in this dark world, and against evil spirits in the heavenly places. Therefore, put on every piece of God's armor so you will be able to resist the enemy in the time of evil. Then after the battle you will still be standing firm. Stand your ground, putting on the belt of truth and the body armor of God's righteousness"* (NLT). Here is what we can learn from this...

Spiritual battles require spiritual strength. The Apostle Paul said, *"A final word: Be strong in the Lord and in His mighty power"* (Ephesians 6:10, NLT). You and I cannot fight the enemy in our own strength. He is too powerful and as human beings we are too weak. The Apostle Paul also said, *"We use God's mighty weapons, not worldly weapons, to knock down the strongholds..."* (2 Corinthians 10:4, NLT). We have access to spiritual weapons for fighting spiritual battles.

Spiritual battles require a spiritual stance. Notice the passage in Ephesians chapter six. It tells us to **"STAND"** three different times. The Apostle Paul stated in Ephesians 6:11, 13 and 14, *"Put on all of God's* *armor so that you will be able to stand firm against all strategies of the devil. Therefore, put on every piece of God's armor so you will be able to resist the enemy in the time of evil. Then after the battle you will still be standing firm. Stand your ground, putting on the belt of truth and the body armor of God's righteousness*" (NLT). After we have prayed, worshipped, declared God's Word, and rebuked the enemy, we need to simply **stand** and **keep on standing**. Standing is our stance against the enemy.

Spiritual battles require a spiritual suit. In Ephesians 10:11 and 13 the Apostle Paul instructs us to, "**Put on all of God's armor** *so that you will be able to stand firm against all strategies of the devil. Therefore, put on every piece of God's armor so you will be able to resist the enemy in the time of evil. Then after the battle you will still be standing firm*" (NLT). Please note that Paul does not instruct us to pick and choose which pieces of armor we want to put on. He does not tell us to just put on parts of the armor. He instructs us to put on the **WHOLE ARMOR**. Why? Because if you leave off any piece of the armor you leave yourself exposed and vulnerable for the enemy to attack and destroy you.

Spiritual battles require spiritual sight. We need to be able to see what the enemy is trying to do in our lives. Paul says in 2 Corinthians 2:11, "*...so that Satan will not outsmart us. For we are* **familiar** *with his evil schemes*" (NLT). If we want to have an advantage over the enemy, we need to learn what his strategies are and be familiar with them. I want to reveal six of the enemy's strategies for you…

1. **Satan wants to DISTRACT you.** He will use problems or even good and exciting things to slowly distract you and pull you away from what God has called you to do. He knows that if he can get you caught up in all the drama that life brings or if he can get you captivated by the "bling bling" or the good and exciting things that life brings, then he can get you off course.

2. **Satan wants to DISCOURAGE you.** He wants to remind you of your past. He wants to make you feel like the situation is hopeless. He wants to make you feel like you are unqualified or unworthy. He knows if he can keep you discouraged, he can keep you from the courage to do what God has called you to do.

3. **Satan wants you to be DISCONTENT.** He wants you to feel like you, your life, or the things in your life are not good enough. He wants you to feel like you have nothing to be happy about in life. He knows that if he can make you discontent with what you have, you will seek out things to satisfy **YOU** rather than seeking God and His plan for your life.

4. **Satan wants you to be DIVIDED.** He wants to separate you from people of like faith. He wants to separate you from positive and joyful people. He wants you to not be unified with anyone because he knows when any two gather or agree, the Lord is there and there is power.

5. **Satan wants you to DOUBT.** He wants you to doubt God's Word, God's promises, God's ability, and God's power. This is because where there is doubt there is no power and where there is faith God's power abounds.

6. **Satan wants to DESTROY you.** He wants to destroy your family, career, health, and your wealth. He wants to destroy your faith because you are a threat to his kingdom!

We need to have the spiritual sight to recognize these strategies when they arise. We must remember that our battle is a spiritual one and our enemy is the devil (Ephesians 6:12), and he is organized, strategic, and he has a plan to defeat you.

THE DEVIL IS A LIAR

Lies are the number one tactic of the enemy. John 8:44 reveals, *"He was a murderer from the beginning. He was always against the truth. There is no truth in him. He is like the lies he tells. Yes, the devil is a liar. He is the father of lies"* (NLT). We give the enemy power when we choose to believe his lies. To believe a lie is to be deceived. When we are deceived, we believe things that are not true. These beliefs keep us from enjoying the life that Jesus died for. Jesus declared in John 10:10, *"I came to give life— life that is full and good"* (NLT). The enemy wants you to believe anything **BUT** this truth! He wants to convince you to believe things that cause you to live beneath your privilege – the life that Jesus paid the price for you to have.

USE YOUR WEAPONS

When we face our enemy, we must use our weapons. We need to know the enemy, but we also need to know our weapons. The Apostle Paul stated in Ephesians 6:13-17, *"Therefore, put on every piece of God's armor so you will be able to resist the enemy in the time of evil. Then after the battle you will still be standing firm. Stand your ground, putting on the belt of truth and the body armor of God's righteousness. For shoes, put on the peace that comes from the Good News so that you will be fully prepared. In addition to all of these, hold up the shield of faith to stop the fiery arrows of the devil. Put on salvation as your helmet, and take the sword of the Spirit, which is the word of God"* (NLT). Here we see Paul use the example of a roman solder to describe the spiritual weapons we can enforce to defeat the enemy. Notice that the only offensive weapon we have is the Sword of the Spirit, which is the Word of God. All the other weapons are defensive, which means our battle position is not to attack but to **STAND** against the enemy. Also note that we are not given anything to cover our back. This is because we are not to run from the enemy. We are to face him and stand our ground. Let's take a closer look at our weapons…

1. The Belt of Truth. Roman soldiers had a belt, and all the other armor was hooked to that belt. When a Roman was preparing for battle, the first thing he did, was gird his loins with that belt. To defend ourselves from the enemy's lies, we must clothe ourselves with truth. The first thing we must do when going into battle is wrap ourselves in the truth. We must know who we are in Christ. We must not rationalize sin. We must know the truth, believe the truth, and live the truth.

2. The Breast Plate of Righteousness. The breastplate is known as the heart protector. It protects the vital organ from destruction. After we have girded ourselves with truth, we must protect our heart with righteousness. No one should dare go into battle without the breastplate. The word "righteousness" in Ephesians chapter six means…

right·eous·ness: |rīCHəsnəs| - *noun*
uprightness or right living; integrity in one's lifestyle and character.

Righteousness is the application of truth in our lives. It is living upright with integrity according to God's Word not according to our own standards or the world's standards. The breastplate guards the heart. If the breastplate represents righteousness, that means that righteousness guards our heart. If you do not apply the truth (God's Word) to your life, I must ask, "What is in your heart?" We must remember that an unprotected heart is asking for some deep, life-threatening wounds.

3. The Shoes of the Gospel of Peace. Roman sandals were strapped up to the knee and tightly fastened to the soldier's leg. The soles had knobs and sometimes nails protruding from them. When soldiers have a firm foundation, they can stand unmoved against their opposition. They do not slip or lose their balance if their feet are gripping the ground. We need to be soldiers with feet solidly planted in certainty. Footing is crucial in the high-stakes, life-or-death war. Without these shoes, we will slip, fall, and find ourselves overwhelmed and defeated. It is pointless to protect our vital organs with truth and righteousness without the right footing. We must be able to support all our equipment with a foundation that will stabilize us and help us keep our backside off the ground. Our foundation should be the Gospel of Peace. The Gospel stabilizes our walk with God. The Gospel is the Good News that Jesus died so we can be saved. This Gospel gives us peace and peace will protect us from doubt. Satan specializes in doubt. He will do anything he can to make you doubt your relationship with God, your salvation, and God's grace (favor) on your life. If he can get you to doubt God and what He has done for you, he can get you to lose your footing in battle.

4. The Shield of Faith. The Roman shield is four feet high and two and a half feet wide. It had hooks on the side to link with the shields of the other soldiers so they could advance without exposing themselves to incoming arrows. Their enemy would set fire to arrows before shooting them at the Romans. The shields were created so that the arrows would pierce the shield deep enough to quench the fire without piercing the soldier or lighting him on fire. This ability to quench arrows that have not only the ability to pierce but to start a destructive fire is what faith does for us in spiritual warfare. Faith in this context means "absolute confidence" in God, His promises, His power, His anointing, and His plan for our lives. The shield's purpose is to quench all the fiery arrows of the enemy. Claiming God's promises by faith, trusting in His unchanging character, and holding up His truth will deflect and extinguish all the enemy's lies, doubt, fear, depression, anger, and oppression. Regardless of the form these incoming flames take, faith always overcomes.

5. The Helmet of Salvation. The last piece of armor a soldier would put on was his helmet. This piece of armor is crucial because if you're hit in the head, you're out. This is an obvious metaphor of the security we have in our salvation, and not just the salvation we have from sin through Jesus. In Ephesians chapter six, salvation means: freedom or deliverance from a threatening enemy. The helmet of salvation is the certainty of deliverance from sin and the protection of our minds in battle. The helmet of salvation helps us to think logically and wisely in a Biblical view. Why is God so concerned about our minds? The mind is the battleground. Many people believe that the war resides in their circumstances, situation, sickness, finance, work, or relationships. Those things are not the priority to the enemy. If the enemy can gain ground on your mind, he can gain ground on all those other areas. If he can distort our thoughts, emotions, and knowledge then the things that make up our life will fall the way he wants them to.

6. The Sword of the Spirit (The Word of God). The Roman soldier also had an enforcer. It was the sword he always had with him. This was not a long heavy sword; it was a light weapon used in close, hand-to-hand combat. It had to be easily accessible and ready to use. The soldier had to be very proficient in using this weapon. How proficient are you with the Word of God? The sword was the only weapon that could be used when the enemy was close. Warriors spent hours upon hours with it in their hands - learning it, getting the feel of it, and letting it become second nature as one of their own limbs. Paul describes what the sword is for us as believers.

WE ARE
NOT
FIGHTING
FOR
VICTORY.

WE ARE
FIGHTING
FROM
VICTORY.

———————

Your sword is the Word of God. Are you learning it, getting the feel of it, and letting it become second nature?

Often in the New Testament, the Greek word for "word" is translated as "logos" which means "the living word". In this scripture, however, it is translated as "rhema" which means, "the specific spoken word" given to us by the Spirit of God. The difference between logos and rhema is the difference between a stockpile of weapons and a sword in a highly skilled hand. The rhema word is the Sword of the Spirit! It is a sharp two edged sword that can divide between the soul and the spirit: between flesh and holiness, between good and evil, between real and unreal, between you and your enemy.

The fact that the Word of God is the Sword of the Spirit teaches two truths. The first truth is that we must have a relationship with the Spirit of God for this weapon to work. The second truth is that we are the soldier who fights with the Sword, but another hand enables it. We must be careful not to use our own authority with the Word but use the authority behind the Word. The Apostle Paul declared, *"For I can do everything* **through Christ***, who gives me strength"* (Philippians 4:13, NLT). It is through His authority that we can win the war. After all, He is the One who has given us the victory. Paul also declared, *"...overwhelming victory is ours* **through Christ***, who loved us"* (Romans 8:37, NLT). It is important for us to live and fight from this truth. We are not fighting **FOR** victory. We are fighting **FROM** victory.

Victory is ours today!

I encourage you to pray this prayer today... *Father, You have already won every battle I will ever face. You are the Lion of the tribe of Judah, and nothing is too hard for You. Through every trial, help me to focus on You. Through every battle, help me to always believe what Your Word says rather than what doubt and fear say. Help me to see myself the way You see me—as a strong, victorious child of God. Lord, I ask You to show me the truth in every area of my life. As I read and study Your Word, please open my eyes to any areas where I am deceived. I want to walk in the good plan You have for my life. Father, thank You for the power of Your*

Word to change me from the inside out. Please continue to change my thoughts and attitudes. Help me to see things from Your perspective. I ask for a fresh desire to read, study, and apply Your Word to every single area of my life. In Jesus' Name. Amen.

EIGHT

LIVE WITH LESS

Be still and know that I am God!
Psalm 46:10 (NLT)

Which of these describes how you have been living your life, handling a particular situation in your life, or viewing a specific aspect of your life: action-less, ambition-less, anchor-less, armor-less, brake-less, care-less, cheer-less, clue-less, comfort-less, compassion-less, direction-less, dream-less, faith-less, goal-less, help-less, hope-less, love-less, order-less, passion-less, point-less, power-less, purpose-less, reck-less, rest-less, result-less, rule-less, sleep-less, smile-less, song-less, standard-less, structure-less, thank-less, thought-less, trust-less, truth-less, virtue-less, vision-less, or weapon-less?

Tell the truth because the truth is the only thing that will set you free. Remember the process: acknowledge it, accept it, and then abort it. We need all the things listed above at some level. There are some things, however, we need to live life with less of. Here are some of those things…

ANGER-LESS

Anger is one letter short of D**ANGER**. In Ecclesiastes 7:9 we are advised to, "*Control your temper, for anger labels you a fool*" (NLT). Have you ever lost your temper and then behaved badly causing you to be regretful or embarrassed? Sadly, I have been there, done that, and bought the t-shirt! There have been times I have lost my temper with people whom I love dearly and have acted like a plain fool! Why? Why do we lose our temper with people we genuinely love? Remember, you cannot bear new fruit until you first deal with the root!

Everyone gets angry. However, we must learn how to control and manage our anger so that it does not get out of hand. If not, anger will control us. Anger does not solve anything. It builds nothing, but it can destroy everything. According to reports from Christian counselors, fifty percent of people who come for counseling have issues with anger management. Out of control anger can destroy communication and relationships. The inability to manage anger can rob you of joy, health, and peace. The problem is that most people want to justify their anger and their bad behavior rather than take responsibility for it. We all struggle with moments of anger. Some more than others. I have good news! God's Word is full of principles that teach us how to manage our anger in a healthy, life giving, and positive way.

When does anger become sin? In Ephesians 4:26 we are advised, "*...do not sin by letting anger control you...*" (NLT). Anger is not a bad thing. It is not wrong to be angry. It is when we let our anger control our thoughts, words, or actions that it becomes sin. In Ephesians 4:15-19 we are told to speak the truth in love and use our words to build up others, not allow rotten or destructive words to pour from our lips.

Choose love and kindness. In Ephesians 4:31-32 we are advised to, "*Get rid of all bitterness, rage, anger, harsh words, and slander, as well as all types of evil behavior. Instead, be kind to each other, tenderhearted, forgiving one another, just as God through Christ has forgiven you*" (NLT). We must first recognize that managing our anger is a choice. We must choose to let love and kindness become stronger than our anger. This is easier said than done, but it can be done. If the person you are angry with is someone near and dear to your heart, let love come in and drive out the anger. If the person you are angry with is your enemy, here is how you handle that: in Romans 12:20-21 Paul tells us, *""If your enemies are hungry, feed them. If they are thirsty, give them something to drink. In doing this, you will heap burning coals of shame on their heads." Do not let evil conquer you but conquer evil by doing good"* (NLT). Our actions are a product of the position of our hearts. The positioning of our hearts can also be altered by our actions. We can change our feelings toward someone by changing how we choose to act toward that person. Instead of killing yourself with bitterness and rage, kill them with kindness. Do all that you can to show them love and kindness. This will not only cleanse you and purge you of negative emotion, but it will bring shame and disgrace upon them for their bad behavior. It is important to remember that it is not about being right. It is about doing what is right and what is right is to show love and kindness, regardless.

Check your pride. Pride is a prison that creates anger and hurt while repelling the restoration that conviction, humility, and reconciliation can bring. As stated earlier, I have lost my temper and acted like a fool with people that I genuinely love. Let's deal with the root. I lost my temper and said or did hurtful things to those I love because they said or did something that hurt me. We tend to put our hurt on other people without even considering how hurt they might be. We make the situation about us. Instead of humbling myself, becoming vulnerable, and communicating appropriately with those people, I let pride get in the way of opening myself up for healing. I responded based on my emotion rather than what I wanted the outcome to be, which was healing. We must remember Proverbs 15:1 which says, *"A gentle answer deflects anger, but harsh words make tempers flare"* (NLT). We must choose our words and responses wisely. Think before you speak. Respond based on what you want the outcome to be not by how you are feeling. If you say something nasty and offensive, own that you said something nasty and offensive. Take responsibility for it. Until you can see that and own it, you cannot heal.

Shut up and listen. James 1:19-20 says, *"Understand this, my dear brothers and sisters: You must all be quick to listen, slow to speak, and slow to get angry. Human anger does not produce the righteousness God desires"* (NLT). Simply put, "shut up and listen." James said that we need to be quick to listen. We are so quick to respond. I have been guilty of formulating my response to a person in my head while they are talking instead of really listening to them. Shut up, even in your mind, and listen. James went on to say that we need to be slow to speak. What James gives us is a formula. If we will be quick to listen and slow to speak, we will be slow to get angry. It is all about listening and thinking before you speak. Our words have power. They can build or they can destroy. Choose and use your words wisely.

Let God handle it. The Apostle Paul teaches us to, *"...never take revenge. Leave that to the righteous anger of God. For the Scriptures say, "I will take revenge; I will pay them back," says the Lord"* (Romans 12:19, NLT). You have this promise when someone wrongs you. What you can do to your enemy cannot compare to what God can do. Learn to let it go, release it to God, and let Him take care of it.

Not all prisons have bars. Some prisons are in your mind. Don't let anger be your prison. Be free! Live anger-less! Next time you feel yourself getting angry, pray this prayer, *"God, give me grace to guard my lips from speaking what is wrong"* (Psalm 141:3, TPT). If you will ask God for help and truly trust Him, He will help you let it go and get through it.

EGO-LESS

EGO. Three letters that keep us from saying things we really need to say, such as: "I love you. I'm sorry. I miss you. I was wrong." Everyone has an ego. We all have the need to feel like we are "somebody". You are somebody because of Jesus; but the moment we think more of ourselves we are facing a huge giant called **PRIDE**. His nickname is **EGO**. Galatians 6:3 says, *"If you think you are too important… you are only fooling yourself. You are not that important"* (NLT).

Pride is a prison. Proverbs 16:18 declares, *"Pride goes before destruction, and haughtiness before a fall"* (NLT). Not only is pride your jailer, but it is also your executioner. Pride kills. We must kill pride before it kills us and every good thing that is in our lives. Careers are destroyed

NOT ONLY IS PRIDE YOUR JAILER, BUT IT IS ALSO YOUR EXECUTIONER.

---

because we are too busy trying to make ourselves "somebody" that we lose the focus and vision required to go to the next level. Marriages and important relationships are destroyed because of pride and ego keeping us from admitting our wrongs, saying we're sorry, and choosing to love and to be kind. When facing a breakdown in a relationship, we often have a list of offenses committed against us by our spouse or loved one. We also usually have a well-rehearsed list of behaviors we expect the person to change. Some people have a list of ways the world around them has failed to serve them in their quest for joy, comfort, and security. The problem is always someone else. Never us. Ego makes you think about what "they" did and how "they" are the problem. When the truth is, we're not willing to forgive someone or have a conversation with someone because we just might have to face the ugly truth and admit the role we played in the breakdown. We must ask ourselves the hard questions and tell the truth. What did I do to cause a breakdown in that relationship? What did I do to push my child away? What did I do to ruin my joy, comfort, or security? Until you tell the truth, you will never heal.

Here are three easy ways to kill ego…

1. **Talk less and listen more.** Stop talking and listen. So many conversations turn into arguments and arguments turn into breakdowns simply because we are too focused on our point of view being heard or because we are too focused on being right. Listen to the other person and then respond.

2. **Be accountable.** Find someone with whom you can process life. You need someone who loves truth and integrity more than they love you and making you feel good. You need someone who will tell you the truth and say, "That right there is pride. Let that go. That attitude is wrong. Make it right."

3. **Accept correction.** When you find that person who tells you the truth, listen to them. Correction makes you better! It hurts. It doesn't feel good. Our ego certainly does not like it, but it develops us into better people. God's Word is an excellent source of correction. 2 Timothy 3:16-17 reminds us that, *"All Scripture is inspired by God and is useful to teach us what is true and to make us realize what is wrong in our lives. It corrects*

us when we are wrong and teaches us to do what is right. God uses it to prepare and equip His people to do every **good work**" (NLT). God's Word is our compass. It is our course correction when we have lost our way. God's Word helps us to "do the work" required for us to heal and be our best selves.

Having an ego is like having something in your eye – without clearing it you can't see clearly. Clear your ego and get a clearer perspective. I encourage you to skip the "e" and let it "go".

FEAR-LESS

Which describes your relationship with the emotion of fear? **F.E.A.R. F**orget **E**verything **A**nd **R**un or **F**ace **E**verything **A**nd **R**ise. Fear has devastating results. It can virtually paralyze an individual and make them helpless because it stops the flow of God's power in their life. Fear is essentially, "wrong believing". Faith and fear both demand that you believe in something you cannot see. Which will you believe?

2 Timothy 1:7 declares, *"For God has not given us a spirit of fear and timidity, but of power, love, and self-discipline"* (NLT). God's plan for us is not fear. Why? Because fear holds us back from being and doing all that God created us for. Fear crushes your spirit and destroys your dreams. Fear stops you from living because everything you want is on the other side of fear.

We all have personal fears. Some of us are afraid of the dark. Some are afraid of heights. Some are afraid of people, while others are afraid of loving. Some of us are afraid of letting go, and others fear trying again. What if I told you that you really aren't afraid of these things at all? That's right. Your fear has lied to you. Here is how fear works. You are not scared of the dark. You fear what might be in the darkness. You are not afraid of heights. You are afraid of the possibility of falling. You are not afraid of the people around you. You are afraid of possible rejection. You are not afraid to love. You are afraid of possibly not being loved in return. You are not afraid to let go. You are afraid to accept the reality that it's gone. You are not afraid to try again. You are afraid of the possibility of failing again. Our fears are based upon "possibilities" or "what might be" or "what might happen". Our fear is just **F**alse **E**vidence **A**ppearing **R**eal. Until we are willing to face those "possibilities" or "what ifs," we will never truly be able to embrace the amazing life Jesus paid the price for us to have. We must remember that fear does not exist anywhere except in the mind.

In Proverbs 3:5-6 you are encouraged to, *"Trust in the Lord with all your heart; do not depend on your own understanding. Seek His will in all you do, and He will show you which path to take"* (NLT). Verse five said, "…do not depend on your own understanding." It tells us this because we cannot trust our own understanding. Our understanding says that there is something to fear in the darkness. Our understanding tells us that if we go higher, we could fall. These things are possibilities, but they are not absolute truths. If we trust in the Lord and seek His will in all we do, then He will lead us and direct us. Fear does not tell you that the darkness you are experiencing is because you are planted, not buried. Fear does not tell you that God is calling you higher and if you slip, He will catch you. Fear does not tell you that God is calling you to let go and that not letting go holds you back from going forward towards the destiny and plan God has for you. We fear getting in the troubled waters, but what fear does not tell us is that God is taking us through the troubled water because our enemy can't swim. Fear leaves out important details. Fear is unreasonable. Fear is a liar. Remember this truth... if God brings you to it, He will bring you through it!

We can have courage knowing what Joshua 1:9 promises, *"This is my command—be strong and courageous! Do not be afraid or discouraged. For the Lord your God is with you wherever you go"* (NLT). We need to understand courage. The difference between fear and courage is that fear is a reaction and courage is a decision. Courage does not mean you aren't afraid. Courage means you have made the decision to not let fear stop you. God does not want us to allow fear to stop us. He is with you. Be bold. Be courageous. Ask yourself this question… What would I do if I wasn't afraid? Then go do that, because everything you want and everything God has for you is on the other side of fear. Winston Churchill said, "Success is not final, failure is not fatal. It is the courage to continue that counts."

VICE-LESS

When I tell you to live your life "vice-less", I'm not talking about the popular 1980's American crime drama television series, "Miami Vice". Here's what I'm talking about living your life with less of…

vice: |*vīs*| - *noun*
an evil, degrading, or immoral practice or habit; a serious moral failing; wicked or evil conduct or habits; corruption; a flaw or imperfection; a defect; a physical defect or weakness; an undesirable habit

Habits are patterns of behavior that are regularly repeated and often occur without any conscious thought. When someone has a habitual behavior, they may not realize it. This is because it has become so routine in their life that it has become a subconscious activity. We don't inherit habits from our parents but rather we learn them as we go through life. From the earliest years of our lives, we have all acquired habits.

We can have good habits and bad habits. We should always remember that habits don't control us; we control the habits. So good habits can be learned, and bad habits can be unlearned. We need to examine all the activities or behaviors in our lives to identify which are bad habits. Bad habits are anything which is seen as a negative or undesirable behavior. Examples of bad habits are sexual immorality, smoking, excessive drinking of alcohol, taking of illegal drugs, gossiping, procrastination, impatience, criticalness, selfishness, tardiness, and so forth. For the follower of God, bad habits are anything that turn our hearts from God and lead us to doing wrong. The only way to overcome a bad habit is by replacing it with a good one.

Here are some examples of how to replace a bad habit with a good one. If your bad behavior is criticism, replace every critical thought or comment with a compliment. If your bad behavior is selfishness, purpose in your mind and heart to perform selfless acts of kindness. This truth is stated in Colossians 3:5-14, "*So put to death the sinful, earthly things lurking within you. Have nothing to do with sexual immorality, impurity, lust, and evil desires. Don't be greedy, for a greedy person is an idolater, worshiping the things of this world. Because of these sins, the anger of God is coming. You used to do these things when your life was still part of this world. But now is the time to get rid of anger, rage, malicious behavior, slander, and dirty language. Do not lie to each other, for you have stripped off your old sinful nature and all its wicked deeds. Put on your new nature, and be renewed as you learn to know your Creator and become like Him… Since God chose you to be the holy people He loves, you must clothe yourselves with tenderhearted mercy, kindness, humility, gentleness, and patience. Make allowance for each other's faults and forgive anyone who offends you. Remember, the Lord forgave you, so you must forgive others. Above all, clothe yourselves with love, which binds us all together in perfect harmony"* (NLT). Putting our sinful nature to death and putting on the new nature is something we must do every day and sometimes from one situation or moment to another. We need to learn to make mercy, kindness, humility, gentleness, patience, and all the other things listed in Colossians 3:5-14 daily habits in our lives. We must purpose in our minds and hearts to make these daily adjustments. You cannot make these changes in your life overnight. It is a daily process. Trust the process. If you don't do well today, try again tomorrow.

Here is the process to replacing your bad habits or behaviors with good ones…

1. **Notice Yourself.** In other words, gain self-awareness. Everything starts with awareness. You must become aware of the moments when you are engaging in the bad habit or behavior. More importantly, try to gain an awareness of the moments right before you act. What is leading you to the habit or behavior? This is called self-observation and it is one of the most powerful life-skills you can develop. Be more aware of your feelings and thoughts because they often lead to actions.

2. **Find the Patterns.** Looking for patterns leads you to discover if the habits or behaviors are triggered by something specific. Search for the triggers. For example, over the past few years I have lost over one hundred pounds. Before I started my weight loss journey, I noticed that if I had a stressful day, I would stop at a fast-food drive-thru or a store and buy more junk food than I could possibly eat in one setting. I did this even if I had

prepared meals at home. I had to learn how to turn to other things during times of stress such as: prayer, scheduled times of relaxation, meditation, etc.

3. **Find the Root.** You cannot bear new fruit until you first deal with the root. Ask yourself the hard questions like… What causes this urge to do something that I know is not good for me? What causes me to react and behave the way I do? Why is that my response? You may find that the root may be tied to something much deeper than what happened before the action or behavior. For example, I mentioned that I would eat junk food after a stressful day. Well, the problem is that every day was pretty much stressful. I had to dig deep on this one and face the hard truths. The root was not stressful days. The root was that during my childhood and teenage years, I developed this unhealthy habit of turning to food to help me process whatever emotion I was dealing with at the time. Food had become my cure-all. Not God. Not His Word. Food. It was what I would turn to when I felt stressed, sad, anxious, or alone. Finding your root may take time and it may be hard work, but it is so worth it.

4. **Reinforce Your Belief.** If you believe nothing will change, then guess what? Nothing is going to ever change. If you choose to reinforce your belief that things can change and that with God's grace you can overcome, you will! Right now, your subconscious belief may be that you need the food, cigarette, alcohol, or other substance to cope with the emotional stuff. Right now, your subconscious belief may be that you need sex to find the validation you never received from your parents. Right now, your subconscious belief is that you need to be critical to protect the fact that you are insecure because you were never told how talented or special you were as a child. Right now, your subconscious belief is that you need to respond with harsh words to protect the broken and hurt seven-year-old child that you really are on the inside. When you are tempted to behave or act wrongly, reinforce your belief that you can change, you are changing, and that you can make a better choice. Then choose!

You won't always get it right. I still have stressful days and there are times that I give in to that "need" for food. Acknowledge that you made a mistake. Then choose to keep going. We don't have to live bound by our bad behavior or habits. We don't have to become victims to the destructive consequences of our bad habits or behaviors. Just choose. Both our sinful nature and our new nature are fighting for control. Which will you choose to allow in the driver's seat of your life?

STRESS-LESS & WORRY-LESS

Conflicts and pressures of life can bring stress and cause worry. Stress and worry are the evidence of our lack of trust in the all-powerful God. They restrict our creative powers and are harmful for our health. We say we trust God, but our worry says another thing. Worry worships the problem. God's Word says for us to rest and trust in Him. As we release stressful matters to the Lord, He can begin to work in the situations that worry and stress us. I have learned and am still learning that God wants me to just sit back, relax (rest), and trust Him to take care of it. He wants me to take my hands off the situation, get out of the way, and let Him work! Even during difficulties, if we can put our focus on Him and praise Him, it will release our tension and stress. The psalmist said, *"Do not worry... Trust in the Lord and do good. Then you will live safely... and prosper. Take delight in the Lord, and He will give you your heart's desires. Commit everything you do to the Lord. Trust Him, and He will help you... Be still in the presence of the Lord and wait patiently for Him to act..."* (Psalm 37:1-7, NLT). Let me break this down for you...

Do not worry. Period. Do not worry. Worry slanders every promise of God and is a total waste of time. It doesn't change anything. We find this wisdom in Proverbs 12:25, *"Worry weighs a person down..."* (NLT). All worry does is steal your joy and keep you very busy doing nothing. I have heard it said that worry is like a rocking chair; it gives you something to do but never gets you anywhere. We need to understand that worrying does not take away tomorrow's troubles. It does, however, take away today's peace. Worrying about how things might go wrong does not help make things go right.

WORRY WORSHIPS THE PROBLEM AND SLANDERS EVERY PROMISE OF GOD.

___

Trust in the Lord and do good. Worry and stress can cause us to do things that are not good for our minds or our bodies. For example, because of stress and worry we start overthinking everything. Overthinking will destroy your happiness and your mood. It will make everything worse than it is. Overthinking causes anxiety because our minds are over worked and need a break. We need to learn to take a deep breath, exhale, and have faith. We also allow stress and worry to cause us to do things that are not healthy for our bodies. We turn to food, drugs, sex, alcohol, cigarettes, and the list goes on. All these things have negative side effects on the bodies God has blessed us with and that we are charged to take care of. We need to stand in this reality: what is going to happen is going to happen and there is nothing we can do about it. Remember that God is in control and that He has promised to make all things work out for your good (Romans 8:28).

Take delight in the Lord, and He will give you your heart's desires. The word, "delight", is a verb. It is an action of taking great pleasure in God, to please Him, or to be His pleasure. When a man's heart is tender toward a woman, in wooing her he will make sure that what he is, does, and says will be pleasing to the woman; he is delighting himself in her. The same applies to delighting ourselves in the Lord. When our hearts are turned towards God, we will want all that we are, do, and say to be pleasing to Him. Hebrews 11:6 says, *"...without faith it is impossible to please Him, for he who comes to God* **must believe that He is**, *and that He is a rewarder of those who diligently seek Him."* (NKJV) It is impossible to please God without faith. Period. We must believe that God is. That He is what? That He is able, faithful, good, our Healer, our Joy, our Peace, our Savior, our Deliverer, etc. We must simply believe that He is whatever we need Him to be and then seek Him. Often, we come to God not seeking Him but seeking what we can receive from Him. I'm not saying that we shouldn't cast our cares on God. We should. He wants us to because He cares for us (1 Peter 5:7). However, every time we come to God it should not be a laundry list of things to do. We need to seek to know Him better and be closer to Him. Just seek Him first and everything else will fall into place (Matthew 6:33).

Commit everything you do to the Lord. What does this mean? It means putting all the heavy lifting on God. Why? Why should we put all the heavy lifting on Him? In Proverbs 16:3, we are given this advice,

"Commit your actions to the Lord, and your plans will succeed" (NLT). When God is in your situation, you cannot fail, and you cannot fall. Allow God to be an active participant in your life by surrendering your plans and agendas over to Him and give Him permission to do what He knows is best for your life and life-circumstances.

Trust Him, and He will help you. How wonderful is this? If we simply trust Him, He will help us. Here are the words of a warrior who truly trusted in the Lord, *"God is our refuge and strength, always ready to help in times of trouble. So, we will not fear when earthquakes come and the mountains crumble into the sea. Let the oceans roar and foam. Let the mountains tremble as the waters surge!"* (Psalm 46:1-3, NLT). When you truly trust in the Lord, this is your anthem. When you truly trust that God is your safety and your help, it does not matter what the situation looks like, what the report is, or what someone said or did. None of it matters because you have confidence that God can, and that He will help you get through whatever you are facing. Trusting in the Lord is taking confidence in Who He is, His Word, and His ability.

Be still in the presence of the Lord and wait patiently for Him to act. Now this is a hard one. We must be still and wait patiently. This isn't fun, but it is totally worth it. Why? Because when we are still and wait, we find strength. We must be still in His presence. We get in His presence through praise and worship (Psalm 22:3). The best way to quiet or still your heart and your mind is by putting your focus on Him through praise and worship. In praise and worship, we are reminded of who God is and what He can do. We must wait patiently for Him to act. Isaiah 40:31 says, *"But those who wait on the Lord, shall renew their strength; They shall mount up with wings like eagles, they shall run and not be weary, they shall walk and not faint"* (NKJV). How do we receive strength from the Lord? We receive it as we wait on Him. The idea behind waiting is not passively sitting around until God does something. In the waiting God wants us to seek and rely on Him instead of our own strength. Our strength changes and is renewed as we seek God through prayer, praise, and reading His Word. Our strength changes and is renewed as we trust God's ability and power instead of our own. This is the kind of strength He gives; it gives us the strength to soar above every worry and care. Therefore, God gives us strength so that we don't have to be stuck, but we can go forward in peace and in power.

Stress and worry touch everyone's life. It is how we respond to the stress and worry that matters. 1 Samuel 30:6 says, "*...David was greatly distressed... but David encouraged himself in the Lord his God*" (KJV). David was stressed out! He was so stressed because his two wives were taken captive and the people were talking about stoning him because they had lost their sons and daughters. What was David's response? He did not panic. He did not worry. Instead, he encouraged himself in the Lord his God. When times of stress come, this should be our response. We need to encourage ourselves. So how do we do this?

1. **Review Your Victories.** It is important in times of stress and worry to remember what the Lord has done for us. This builds our faith in God's ability to work in our current situation. The psalmist gives us a great example of this when He says in Psalm 77:1-12, "*I cry out to God; yes, I shout. Oh, that God would listen to me! When I was in deep trouble, I searched for the Lord. All night long I prayed, with hands lifted toward heaven, but my soul was not comforted. I think of God, and I moan, overwhelmed with longing for His help. You don't let me sleep. I am too distressed even to pray! ...Has the Lord rejected me forever? Will He never again be kind to me? Is His unfailing love gone forever? Have His promises permanently failed? Has God forgotten to be gracious? Has He slammed the door on His compassion? And I said, "This is my fate; the Most High has turned His hand against me."* **BUT THEN** *I recall all You have done, O Lord; I remember Your wonderful deeds of long ago. They are constantly in my thoughts. I cannot stop thinking about Your mighty works*" (NLT). Have you ever felt like this psalmist? I have. I have felt hopeless and like God had turned His back on me, **BUT THEN** I remember all that God has done for me in my life and my faith is encouraged because I know that if He did it before, He can do it again.

2. **Remember Who You Are and Whose You Are.** Stop everything you are doing. Stop pacing the floor. Stop planning.

Stop rehearsing those negative, hopeless thoughts in your head. Stand still. Take a deep breath and remember. You are a child of the Creator of the universe. Nothing is too hard or too big for Him. He has a plan and a purpose for you and for every event or circumstance that happens in your life. God said in Jeremiah 29:11, *"For I know the plans I have for you," says the Lord. "They are plans for good and not for disaster, to give you a future and a hope"* (NLT). And that right there is all you need to know. You are not a victim of your circumstances. Problems do not happen **TO** you; they happen **FOR** you. Every life-event has come to mold you and shape you into the mighty warrior God has called you and created you to be. Defeat is not a part of the plan. Victory is yours because He loves you! The Apostle Paul declared, *"Does it mean He no longer loves us if we have trouble or calamity, or are persecuted, or are hungry, or destitute, or in danger, or threatened with death? ...No, despite all these things, overwhelming victory is ours through Christ, who loved us"* (Romans 8:35-37, NLT).

3. **Regroup and Refocus.** It is important to pause and fix our thoughts in times of stress and worry. If not, we will find ourselves overwhelmed and without peace. Isaiah 26:3 declares, *"You will keep in perfect peace all who trust in You, all whose thoughts are fixed on You!"* (NLT). We must shift our focus from the problem and put it on the Problem Solver. This is the only way we can maintain peace in troubling times.

4. **Remember God's Word.** In our moments of stress and worry it is important to stop and remember God's Word. His Word is truth, and it is full of His thoughts, plans, and promises for our lives and every situation we face. The psalmist declared in Psalm 33:4, *"The Lord's word is true, and He is faithful in everything He does"* (ERV). We can stand on this promise and every other promise listed in His Word because, *"God is not a man; He will not lie. God is not a human being; His decisions will not change. If He says He will do something, then He will do it. If He makes a promise, then He will do what He promised"* (Numbers 23:19,

ERV). Stand on His Word and you will not fail or fall. It is an anchor and a firm foundation for our lives.

5. **Reward Yourself.** Give yourself a break! Life is all about balance. You don't always need to be getting, gaining, achieving, or mastering. Sometimes it is perfectly okay and necessary to shut down, kick back, and do nothing. Take some time to rest and recover. It's okay if the only thing you do today is breath. Breathing is not overrated. Step back from the busyness and take care of yourself. Those moments of self-care will add value, energy, purpose, and creativity to everything you do. Find a balance and enjoy your life!

Living with less is easier said than done, but it can be done. The way you do it is by making the deliberate choice each day to live with less anger, ego, fear, bad behaviors or habits, stress, and worry. Take baby steps. Every step counts. The more you do the work, the more you will find real lasting change in your life.

Choose to embrace the amazing and abundant life Jesus paid the price for you to live.

NINE

THE GIFT OF GOODBYE

*...Let us strip off every weight that slows us down,
especially the sin that so easily trips us up...*
Hebrews 12:1-2 (NLT)

Hebrews chapter twelve encourages us to let go of anything in our lives that slows us down. In other words, give yourself the gift of goodbye. Say goodbye to sin, the past, unhealthy relationships, and negative mindsets. Let it all go…

SAY GOODBYE TO YESTERDAY

The past can mess you up and hold you in bondage if you try to bring it into your future. Do not let the past chain you, bind you, and imprison you. Do not let it hold you back and keep you from going forward. You are either a prisoner of your past or a pioneer of your future; the choice is yours. Don't let the voice of yesterday delay your process. Don't let the voice of yesterday define your tomorrow – your future. Where you have been does not determine where you're going. The Apostle Paul said in Philippians 3:13-14, "*No, dear brothers and sisters, I have not achieved it, but I focus on this one thing:* **Forgetting the past and looking forward to what lies ahead**, *I press on to reach the end of the race and receive the heavenly prize for which God, through Christ Jesus, is calling us*" (NLT). Forget the past and go forward.

Look at Paul's life as an example of saying goodbye to yesterday. Paul used to be called, "Saul." Saul persecuted Christians. Acts chapter eight verse three reveals that Saul traveled from place to place doing all he could to destroy the church. He dragged people out of their homes and threw them in prison. This was Paul's yesterday. This was his reputation. In Acts chapter nine, Saul's story is interrupted by Jesus and his life is completely and radically transformed. Before this interruption happened to Saul's story, Saul goes before the high priest for legal authorization to persecute Christians. On his way to Damascus, light shines around him and from the light he hears a voice speak, "Saul! Saul! Why are you persecuting me?" Saul asks, "Who are you?" The voice replies, "I am Jesus, the one you are persecuting! Now get up and go into the city, and you will be told what you must do." Saul stands up, opens his eyes, and realizes that he is blind. The men who were with him helped him to Damascus where he remained blind for three days. Jesus interrupted Saul's story. Just that quick, Saul's life turns around. Sometimes we need to lose sight of where we are headed for our vision and perspective to be renewed and redirected.

Jesus then appears to a man in Damascus named, Ananias. He tells Ananias that he must go to Saul and pray for him so that he can receive back his sight because Saul was His chosen instrument to share His message. Ananias lays his hands on Saul and Saul is healed. Saul begins preaching in the synagogues that Jesus is the Son of God. The people in the town began to talk about Saul, "Is this not the same man who caused such devastation among Jesus' followers in Jerusalem?" That is exactly how people will treat you. When you start living differently, people will bring up your past. Don't let your past keep you from being who God is calling you to be and what He is calling you to do. God said in Jeremiah 29:11, "*'For I know the plans I have for you,' says the Lord. 'They are plans for good and not for disaster, to give you a future and a hope'*" (NLT). God is focused on your future, not your past. He cares more about where you are going and not where you have been. God can and will use your story for His glory. It doesn't matter what your past was, what you have been through, the mistakes you have made, or how you have lived. Repent, give it to God, and go forward. Remember, you are either a prisoner of your past or a pioneer of your future.

By releasing yesterday and embracing his tomorrow, Saul was empowered with **NEW VISION**. The Bible says that the scales fell from his eyes. His perspective changed. His outlook shifted. By letting go of yesterday and embracing his tomorrow, Saul was given a **NEW REPUTATION**. He is one of the greatest teachers that ever lived, and He wrote most of the New Testament. By letting go of yesterday and embracing his tomorrow, Saul was given a **NEW IDENTITY**. The Lord gave him a new name, Paul. He was never the same again.

The same is possible for you when you make the choice to say goodbye to yesterday and embrace your destiny! The Apostle Paul declared, *"Therefore, if any man be in Christ, he is a new creature: old things are passed away; behold, all things are become new"* (2 Corinthians 5:17 KJV). Do you believe this? If so, then don't let yesterday keep you from being successful in God today. Don't worry about the past. If anyone is in Christ, he is a new creature - a new person regardless of any addiction, negative situation, or bad life-choices! Whenever the voice of yesterday tries to hold you back or trip you up and make you feel unqualified and disqualified for the destiny God is calling you to, I want you to remember this… Jacob was a cheater, Peter denied Jesus, David had an affair, Moses was a murderer, Noah got drunk, Jonah ran from God, Paul persecuted Christians, and Rahab was a prostitute. Each of these people had a past and God used every one of them! Do not let past labels limit the future God has for you!

God does not call the qualified, He qualifies the called.

This is what we are commanded to do and what we are promised, *"So do not remember what happened in earlier times. Do not think about what happened a long time ago because I am doing something new! Now*

YOU ARE EITHER A PRISONER OF YOUR PAST OR A PIONEER OF YOUR FUTURE.

---

you will grow like a new plant. Surely you know this is true. I will even make a road in the desert, and rivers will flow through that dry land" (Isaiah 43:18-19 ERV). Forget about where you have been. Focus on where you are going. Focus on what God is wanting to do in you and through you. Let God lead you and watch Him do the impossible!

SAY GOODBYE TO THE LIDS

Your life is built by relationships. Those closest to you help determine the course of your life. Your relationships shape who you are and where you're going. The people you allow into your life; the people you allow to influence your thinking and your choices shape you. We read in Proverbs 27:17, *"As iron sharpens iron, so a friend sharpens a friend"* (NLT). If your relationships can make you sharper, they can make you weaker. Relationships really do shape your world. I have heard it said that people are like elevators. Some take you up and some take you down.

In Genesis chapter thirteen we find Abram leaving Egypt with his wife, his nephew Lot, and all their possessions. The land was not big enough for Abram's and Lot's possessions. This caused an argument between Abram's and Lot's men. Abram told Lot, *"Let's not allow this conflict to come between us or our herdsmen... The whole countryside is open to you. Take your choice of any section of the land you want, and we will separate..."* (Genesis 13:8-9, NLT). Lot surveyed the land and noticed the plain of Jordan was well watered and chose that place. Abram lived in Canaan and Lot lived near Sodom. God called Abram to another level of living and told him to leave everything behind. Abram chose to bring his nephew Lot who benefited from the level Abram was living in, but Lot did not contribute to it. The meaning of "Lot" is "to cover". Lot's presence covered or put a lid on what Abram could achieve. While God blessed Abram and increased him, there came a time when Abram needed to separate from Lot. After Abram said, "Goodbye" to Lot, God spoke to Abram, *" 'Look as far as you can see in every direction... I am giving you all this land... to you and your descendants as a permanent possession...' "* (Genesis 13:14-17, NLT). Abram needed to move away from Lot so that he could move up!

We have this promise, *"The Lord shall increase you more and more, you and your children"* (Psalm 115:14, KJV). Are there people you need to move away from so that you can move up into the "more and more" God has for you? I'm not necessarily talking about physically moving away from them, but emotionally. If the people around you are living with limits, they are placing those same limits on you. These limits could be narrow mindsets, low expectations, even selfish motives, or so many other things. There are some people that don't expect anything from you. They do not expect you to grow, so they will never speak to your potential. They want you to stay where you are so they can justify remaining where they are. Perhaps they don't want you to know how smart and talented you are so they can take advantage of your gifts. There are people that limit you and you can feel it. You have grown and prospered, and they want to treat you as if you have not. Sometimes it is the culture in which you are living. Think of Jesus returning to His hometown (in Mark 6:5-6) where, *"He could do no mighty work...because of their unbelief."* And in John 1:46 where they said (about Jesus), *"Can anything good come out of Nazareth?"* (KJV).

Therefore, God told Abraham that He would not take him further until he eliminated the lids. God wanted to give Abraham an open heaven and do mighty works in his life, but Abraham needed to remove himself from people that were limiting and restricting him. To step into a new station in life, we must first re-station ourselves. Many of us have grown and God is wanting to promote us to another level of success and abundance or of increased capacity, influence, and position. Be willing to walk away from those limiters who restrict you and take the lid off your potential. Give yourself the gift of goodbye and say "hello" to your new season!

You may be holding on to a hurt that was caused by someone who left you. When people can walk away from you, let them walk! Don't try to talk another person into staying with you, loving you, calling you, caring about you, coming to see you, or staying attached to you. Your destiny is not, never has been, and never will be tied to anybody that leaves you. We read in 1 John 2:19, *"They left us, but they were never really with us. If they had been, they would have stuck it out with us, loyal to the end. In leaving, they showed their true colors, showed they never did belong"* (MSG). People leave you because they are not joined to you, and if they are not joined to you, you cannot make them stay. It does not always mean they are a bad person. It just means that their part in the story is over and that is okay! You have got to acknowledge when a person's part in your story is over. Do not keep trying to raise the dead. Let them go!

Pursue people who motivate your obedience. Connect with people who are guided by their character. Stay in relationship with people who defend you in your absence. Lock arms with people who fear God more than they love you. Hang out with people who motivate you to sow and be generous. Stand with people who have been assigned to your future and unlock your gratitude. Do this and watch your life go higher!

SAY GOODBYE TO STINKIN' THINKIN'

Our lives are a product of our thoughts. The Apostle Paul tells us to think great thoughts. In Philippians 4:8-9 he says, *"Fix your thoughts on what is true, honorable, right, pure, lovely, and admirable. Think about things that are excellent and worthy of praise..."* The command is to "think" about these things. The mind is where we think, feel, and decide. It is the place where all the conflicts of life begin. It is the ultimate battlefield of life. God, our flesh, and the devil are all battling for control of our minds. The battle rages in our minds because, *"For as he thinks in his heart, so is he."* (Proverbs 23:7, NKJV) The devil knows that if He can corrupt your thinking, he can corrupt your living. We do not have to live defeated by wrong thinking. There are hundreds of promises in God's Word. Stand on them!

You must give yourself a check-up from the neck-up from time to time. In James 4:7 we are told to, *"Submit to God and resist the devil..."* (KJV). We must submit our mindsets to the spirit of God. His Spirit will daily renew your mind and help you close the door on stinkin' thinkin'.

We do not have to live defeated by wrong thinking. 1 Peter 1:13-16 says, *"So roll up your sleeves, get your head in the game, be totally ready [hope] to receive the gift that's coming when Jesus arrives. Do not lazily slip back into those old grooves of evil, doing just what you feel like doing. You did not know any better then; you do now. As obedient children, let yourselves be pulled into a way of life shaped by God's life, a life energetic and blazing with holiness. God said, "I am holy; you be holy"'* (MSG). As we get a grip on our thoughts, we get in position for God's ministering Spirit and His Word to renew and wash our minds so that we can then *"be totally ready [hope] to receive the gift..."* God has for us.

Even if the road is hard, we can have hope because God promised:
- that our path is planned. (Psalm 37:23)
- to make all things work for our good. (Romans 8:28)
- to go with us through everything in life. (Hebrews 13:5)
- that we would abide in victory. (1 Corinthians 15:57 and Romans 8:37)
- our destiny will be worth every mile. (Romans 8:18 and 2 Corinthians 4:17)

Forget the former things. Don't even consider how things used to be. God wants to do a new thing in your mind, heart, and life right now! Will you let Him? You must be willing to lose it all to gain so much more. Say, "goodbye". Let go of the past, the lids, and stinkin' thinkin'. It is the greatest gift you could ever give yourself!

TEN

THINK ABOUT WHAT YOU'RE THINKING ABOUT

... Fix your thoughts on what is true, and honorable, and right, and pure, and lovely, and admirable. Think about things that are excellent and worthy of praise.
Philippians 4:8 (NLT)

Life is full of frustrating moments: bad news, fake news, sickness, isolation, fear, anger, financial worries, struggles, relationship breakdowns, the list goes on. You know what else frustrates us? Not trusting God. Trying to do something that isn't working, that is never going to work because it isn't God's plan also frustrates us. Other sources of frustration are trying to control things beyond our control, being in relationships with people we have no business being in relationship with, attempting to do things in our own strength, and doing things we are not called to do. Do you want peace in your life? It's simple. If God is not in it, get out of it! If He isn't in that relationship, plan, idea, mindset, or "thing" then get out of it.

To be frustrated is to be angry, stressed, depressed, anxious, lacking peace or rest. Frustration has everything to do with our minds. The mind is the battlefield. We need to recognize frustration for what it is. Frustration positions us to be manipulated by the enemy. The enemy takes advantage of our moments of frustration. He takes anger and stress and twists it until you are in a state of anxiety or depression. Before you know it, he has robbed you of your peace that Jesus paid the high price for you to have! We all have moments of frustration. Frustration knocks on the door of life for everyone, but here is the good news…

WE DO NOT HAVE TO LIVE FRUSTRATED

Jesus did not just die so we could go to heaven someday. He died so we can enjoy life. Jesus revealed in John 10:10, *"The thief's (Satan's) purpose is to steal and kill and destroy. My purpose is to give them a rich and satisfying life"* (NLT). Jesus came and paid the price for each one of us to live an abundant, amply supplied, plentiful, exceptional, extraordinary, and remarkable life. If these words do not describe the life you're living, you are living beneath your privilege.

We cannot enjoy life if we're always frustrated. Here is a little life hack for you: you can't get frustrated if you refuse to submit to the thoughts that bombard your mind. You don't have to believe everything that you think. By overthinking, we often create problems that aren't even there. I admit that I can ponder a thing and roll it over and over in my mind until I start feeling confused and frustrated or worried and anxious. I have learned that I have two options. I can either ponder on something until I start losing my peace or I can choose to trust who God is and trust His plan for my life. We must know God and His character to trust who He is. The best way to get to know Him is to get in His word and study it. John 1:1 declares, *"In the beginning the Word already existed. The Word was with God, and the Word was God"* (NLT). God is His word. By reading and studying it we get to know Him and His character. We get to see things from His perspective and point of view. We get to see His heart for ourselves. Plain and simple. No guessing. No wondering. To trust His plan for our lives we must truly believe that He has plan and a purpose for everything we face or walk through and that it is for our good. We must truly believe that His plan and purpose for our lives is far greater than our past or our circumstances.

I was addicted to reasoning. I had to "think" I had it all figured out. I had to "think" I knew what God was going to do and how He was going to do it. All I did was think, think, think, think, think. Before I knew it, I was frustrated, worried about what could be, doubting if God would, and having anxiety attacks. Thinking is not overrated. We need to think before speaking and we need to think before we do certain things. However, the enemy uses our human reasoning against us. It has been his strategy from the beginning in the garden of Eden. Genesis 3:1-6 reveals this to us, *"The serpent was the shrewdest of all the wild animals the Lord God had made. One day he asked the woman, "Did God really say you must not eat the fruit from any of the trees in the garden?" "Of course, we may eat fruit from the trees in the garden," the woman replied. "It's only the fruit from the tree in the middle of the garden that we are not allowed to eat. God said, 'You must not eat it or even touch it; if you do, you will die.'" "You won't die!" the serpent replied to the woman. "God knows that your eyes will be opened as soon as you eat it, and you will be like God, knowing both good and evil."* **The woman was convinced.** *She saw that the tree was beautiful, and its fruit looked delicious, and she wanted the wisdom it would give her. So, she took some of the fruit and ate it. Then she gave some to her husband, who was with her, and he ate it, too"* (NLT).

Satan reasoned with Eve so that she would be enticed to believe him – to believe his lie. Verse six shows us how she started reasoning within herself. I am sure she thought to herself, "The fruit is beautiful, and it sure looks delicious. Not to mention, it is going to make me wise." The enemy used her human reasoning against her. This is what he does with you and me. He uses our human reasoning to convince us to believe his lies. He watches us, he tells us lies, and he entices us so that we will begin to reason why our sin, negative thought pattern, bad behavior, addiction, anger, etc. are okay.

SATAN'S STRATEGY

2 Corinthians 10:4-5 declares, "*We use God's mighty weapons, not worldly weapons, to knock down the strongholds of human reasoning and to destroy false arguments. We destroy every proud obstacle that keeps people from knowing God. We capture their rebellious thoughts and teach them to obey Christ*" (NLT). We cannot just hold on to and reason with whatever falls into our head. Satan offers wrong thinking to everyone. We don't have to accept his offer. The enemy uses our mind, our thoughts, and our reasoning to tell us things about ourselves, others, and circumstances that just are not true.

> **rea·son·ing:** | *ˈrēz(ə)niNG*| - *verb*
> to think, understand, and form judgments by a process of logic *(humans do not reason entirely from facts or truth)*

As human beings, we do not reason from the facts or the truth. We like to reason from what we see, what we feel, or what we hear. We must learn to reason from the truth of God's Word. What does God's Word say about you? What does God's Word say about your situation or circumstance?

> **rea·son·ing:** | *ˈrēz(ə)niNG*| - *verb*
> to find an answer to a problem by considering various possible solutions.

So instead of trusting God, we innocently try to fix our problem by considering the various possible solutions. The enemy uses this against us. Let me be clear. I'm not saying that problem solving skills are bad. I'm not saying that we should not think. However, the enemy does use the gift of problem solving and human reasoning against us. Therefore, we must do what 2 Corinthians 10:4-5 tells us to do. We must capture our thoughts and teach them to obey Christ so that the gifts of problem solving and human reasoning are used appropriately and responsibly.

The enemy is strategic in how he uses our minds against us. He does not hit us once with a thought or a lie. No! He bombards our mind with a cleverly devised pattern of little nagging thoughts, suspicions, doubts, fears,

SATAN OFFERS WRONG THINKING TO EVERYONE. WE DON'T HAVE TO ACCEPT HIS OFFER.

wonderings, reasonings, and theories. We saw this in the beginning with Eve in Genesis chapter three. He moves slowly and cautiously. He has a strategy for his warfare. What's your strategy?

OUR STRATEGY

We are given our strategy in 2 Corinthians 10:4-5. Verse four says, *"We use God's mighty weapons, not worldly weapons, to knock down the strongholds of human reasoning and to destroy false arguments"* (NLT). Our strategy is that we use God's mighty weapons. Let me be clear. This is the only winning strategy…

Prayer is a mighty weapon. In Mark 9:25-29 we read, *"When Jesus saw that the crowd of onlookers was growing, He rebuked the evil spirit. "Listen, you spirit that makes this boy unable to hear and speak," He said. "I command you to come out of this child and never enter him again!" Then the spirit screamed and threw the boy into another violent convulsion and left him. The boy appeared to be dead. A murmur ran through the crowd as people said, "He's dead." But Jesus took him by the hand and helped him to his feet, and he stood up. Afterward, when Jesus was alone in the house with His disciples, they asked Him, "Why couldn't we cast out that evil spirit?" Jesus replied, "This kind can be cast out only by prayer""* (NLT). What we learn from this story is simple. There are some things that can only be moved by prayer.

Praise and worship is a mighty weapon. King David exclaimed in Psalm 144:1, *"Praise the Lord, who is my rock. He trains my hands for war and gives my fingers skill for battle"* (NLT). David was a musician. He was a worshipper. When he wrote the psalms, he wrote them as songs and hymns of praise. I want you to imagine David playing his harp with his hands and fingers as he is singing this hymn of praise to God. He said, *"He trains my hands for war and gives my fingers skill for battle."* He is acknowledging that God was using his praise and worship as a weapon of warfare against his enemy. Your praise and worship is a powerful weapon.

His Word is our greatest weapon. We must line up our thoughts with God's thoughts. His Word is His thoughts. So, we must line up our thoughts with God's Word. 2 Corinthians 10:4-5 declares, *"We use God's mighty weapons, not worldly weapons, to knock down the strongholds of human reasoning and to destroy false arguments. We destroy every proud obstacle that keeps people from knowing God. We capture their rebellious thoughts and teach them to obey Christ"* (NLT). When those nagging thoughts, suspicions, and doubts creep in. When those fears, wonderings, or anxiety pop up. When those reasonings and theories start, put the Word to it! What do I mean? When those thoughts creep in that are contrary to your knowledge of God, His character, and His Word, capture those thoughts, use God's mighty weapons, and teach them to obey Christ. Simply put… Stop them in their tracks, put the Word to it, and make them obey the Spirit!

For example: When you have thoughts such as…

- *It's impossible!*
  THINK ON: Matthew 19:26 which tells us that with God all things are possible.

- *You can't!*
  THINK ON: Philippians 4:13 which tells us that we can do all things through Christ who gives us strength.

- *Worry! Be afraid!*
  THINK ON: 2 Timothy 1:7 which tells us that God has not given us a spirit of fear but power, love, and a sound mind.

- *You're alone!*
  THINK ON: Hebrews 13:5 which tells us that God said, "I will never leave you, nor turn My back on you."

- *You aren't loved! You aren't loveable!*
  THINK ON: Romans 8:38-39 which tells us that neither death, nor life, nor angels, nor principalities, nor powers, nor things present, nor things to come, nor height, nor depth, nor any other creature, can separate us from the love of God, which is in Christ Jesus our Lord.

- *Everyone is against you!*
  THINK ON: Romans 8:31 which tells us that if God be for us, who can be against us?

- *You can't be forgiven for your past!*
  THINK ON: 1 John 1:9 which tells us that if we confess our sins, He is faithful and just to forgive us of our sins, and to cleanse us from all unrighteousness.

- *This situation is going to end badly!*
  THINK ON: Romans 8:28 which tells us that all things work out for the good of them that love God and are called according to His purpose.

- *God will not come through for you!*
  THINK ON: Numbers 23:19 which tells us that God is not a man, so He does not lie. He is not human, so He does not change His mind. It then asks us, *"Has He ever spoken and failed to act? Has He ever promised and not carried it through?"* (NLT)

- *This thing is going to take you out!*
  THINK ON: Isaiah 54:17 which promises that no weapon that is formed against us will prosper; and every word that is spoken against us will not succeed. Please note that it does not promise that weapons would not be formed against us. It does not promise that words will not be spoken against us. No! They will, but they will not prosper or succeed.

Make those thoughts and lies submit and obey the truth of God's Word. There is a truth for every lie the enemy throws at you. The key to responding to his lies with the truth is knowing the truth. John 8:31-32 tells us that, *"Jesus said to the people who believed in Him, "You are truly My disciples if you remain faithful to My teachings. And you will know the truth, and the truth will set you free ""* (NLT). The truth is what will set you free, but the key is you must know the truth. Jesus told His disciples how we know the truth; we must remain faithful to His teachings. The way we do that is by renewing our minds everyday with the Word of God through personal reading and devotion. When we do that, we will have His truth in our minds and hearts, and we can live free from every lie of the enemy. We will have an entire arsenal of weapons ready to pull out and use to combat the lies of the enemy. The choice is ours. We can obey our thoughts and the lies of the enemy. Or we can obey the truth of His Word. Which will you choose?

IT IS IMPOSSIBLE TO WORRY AND LIVE IN PEACE AT THE SAME TIME

anx·i·e·ty: |*aNG'zīədē*|
noun. a feeling of worry, nervousness, or unease, typically about an imminent event or something with an uncertain outcome – *verb*. tormenting oneself with disturbing thoughts

We're smarter than that. Worrying, being afraid, and being frustrated changes nothing. So why not give it up?

wor·ry: | *'warē*| - *verb*
to give way to anxiety or unease; to allow one's mind to dwell on difficulty or troubles; to tear at, gnaw on, or drag around with the teeth…

This is what the enemy does to us with worry and anxiety. He tears at us and gnaws at us. This is how we feel after hours of repeated worry and anxiety. We feel like we have been dragged around. This is what Jesus has to say about worry, "*That is why I tell you not to worry about everyday life— whether you have enough food and drink, or enough clothes to wear. Isn't life more than food, and your body more than clothing? Look at the birds. They don't plant or harvest or store food in barns, for your heavenly Father feeds them. And aren't you far more valuable to Him than they are? Can all your worries add a single moment to your life? "And why worry about your clothing? Look at the lilies of the field and how they grow. They don't work or make their clothing, yet Solomon in all his glory was not dressed as beautifully as they are. And if God cares so wonderfully for wildflowers that are here today and thrown into the fire tomorrow, He will certainly care for you. Why do you have so little faith? "So, do not worry about these things, saying, 'What will we eat? What will we drink? What will we wear?' These things dominate the thoughts of unbelievers, but your heavenly Father already knows all your needs. Seek the Kingdom of God above all else, and live righteously, and He will give you everything you need. "So don't worry about tomorrow, for tomorrow will bring its own worries. Today's trouble is enough for today"* (Matthew 6:25-34, NLT). To put it simply: Believers are not dominated by worry. Believers seek God first, live right, and everything else falls into place. That is a promise, and we can live in peace knowing this truth.

THE FIVE STEP PROGRAM

The Apostle Paul gives us a five-step program for getting our thoughts under control and walking in peace. This five-step program is found in Philippians 4:4-9.

STEP ONE. Paul says, *"Be cheerful with joyous celebration in every season of life. Let your joy overflow! Do not be pulled in different directions or worried about a thing"* (Philippians 4:4 & 6a, NLT). **Choose joy regardless of where you are or what is happening in your life.** Don't be jerked around by your emotions such as worry, fear, anger, or anxiety. Why should we choose joy regardless of our situation or circumstance? The Word teaches us that joy is our strength. Nehemiah 8:10 declares, *"...for the joy of the Lord is your strength."* (NLT). Joy gives us the strength to get through whatever we're facing. We must not confuse joy with happiness. Joy is an inner feeling. Happiness is an outward expression. Joy endures hardship and trials and connects with meaning and purpose. A person pursues happiness but chooses joy. Let me make something clear, it is not your spouse's job to make you happy. It is not your friend's job or your boss's job to make you happy. Your happiness is your business. It is an inside job. It is a choice. Choose to be happy. Choose joy.

STEP TWO. Paul says, *"Be saturated in prayer throughout each day, offering your faith-filled requests before God with overflowing* *gratitude. Tell Him every detail of your life, then God's wonderful peace that transcends human understanding, will guard your heart and mind through Jesus Christ"* (Philippians 4:6b-7, NLT). **Pray about everything.** We should pray about everything that happens in our lives or that concerns us because prayer is how we give our cares and burdens to the Lord. We are advised in 1 Peter 5:7 to, *"Give all your worries and cares to God, for He cares about you"* (NLT).

STEP THREE. Paul says, *"Keep your thoughts continually fixed on all that is authentic and real, honorable and admirable, beautiful and respectful, pure and holy, merciful and kind"* (Philippians 4:8a, NLT). **Fix your thoughts continually.** We need to work to fix our thoughts on a regular basis because we are advised in 1 Peter 5:8 to, *"Stay alert! Watch out for your great enemy, the devil. He prowls around like a roaring lion, looking for someone to devour"* (NLT). We can't possibly be aware of the enemy and his attacks if we are distracted by out-of-control thinking.

STEP FOUR. Paul says, *"And fasten your thoughts on every glorious work of God, praising Him always"* (Philippians 4:8b, NLT). **Praise God for what He has already done in your life.** This is important because praise brings God into our situation. The psalmist declares in Psalm 22:3, *"Yet You are holy, enthroned on the praises of Israel"* (NLT). When we praise, we basically pull up a chair and invite God to come sit with us right where we are. Your praise invites God in and in His presence is the fullness of everything you need.

STEP FIVE. Paul says, *"Put into practice the example of all that you have heard from me or seen in my life and the God of peace will be with you in all things"* (Philippians 4:9, NLT). **Live right.** It's just that simple. Apply the Word of God to your life and live it. When we do this, peace will be with us always.

Your mind plays an important role in your victory.

The enemy knows if he can defeat your thinking, he can defeat every other area of your life. It is imperative that we never ever give up. Putting a stop to negative thought patterns that we have lived with our entire lives and creating new ways of thinking is hard work. We must commit and be willing to do that work. We must always remember that the more we change our mind for the better the more our lives will change for the better.

ELEVEN

PEACE NOT PIECES

...Search for peace, and work to maintain it.
Psalm 34:14 (NLT)

Everyone goes through something. That something could be internal, mental, emotional, or physical. It could be something in our work or our relationships. Everyone goes through something that makes them look at themselves and say, "Okay, this just isn't working." It could be extra weight, the way you live, the way you speak, the way you process life, how you handle certain situations, the way you think, or the way you feel. How do we get through what we're going through and come out better than when we went in? We start by looking at the broken pieces of our lives.

GENERATIONAL CURSES

Many of our broken pieces stem from generational curses. Generational curses are something we inherit. That's right. We inherit things from people known and unknown, seen and unseen in our families.

We go through life with a broken state of our identity, and we don't understand where it has originated. These generational curses take certain things from us and give certain things to us. Your family's generational curse might teach you that because you are a woman you do not matter as much as a man or that your voice does not matter. Your generational curse might teach you that because of your race you will never succeed. Your generational curse could teach you that because you come from a certain economic background you will never get out of a certain part of town. It doesn't matter how successful, educated, or wealthy you may be, your identity is infected by these generational curses.

To achieve peace, we must understand generational curses. A generational curse is the cumulative effect on a person of things that their ancestors did, believed, or practiced in the past, and a consequence of an ancestor's actions, beliefs, and sins being passed down. We must go through and study the causes and effects of the broken pieces in our lives. Many unknowingly, walk around living out generational curses that we have inherited from the people and experiences of our past. It could be a generational curse of poverty, a lack of education, working very hard and receiving very little, addiction, lack of vision, abuse, hereditary disease, divorce, domestic violence, adultery, perversion, depression, confusion, fear, panic attacks, mental illness, suicide, destructive attitudes, and behaviors. The list goes on. From that generational curse grows a pattern of behavior that we practice throughout our lives every day.

Most of us have become comfortable with the chaos in our lives. Chaos is "normal" for us. The generational curse that has created the chaos leads us into patterns of behavior that convinces us that there is no way out or this is just how life is meant to be even though it is hurting or dishonoring us. You must be clear about who you are and what you really want. If not, you will continue to live in the cycle of chaos. It is up to you to break the generational curses. When they say, "It runs in the family." You say, "This is where it runs out!" It ran in your family until it ran into you! God says, "You have been anointed to break the cycle!" Generational curses stop with you! Declare that and believe it. You can move from broken pieces to peace if you will stop telling stories that are not true about who you are and what you need.

You can move from broken pieces to peace if you will stop being a terrorist in your own mind – terrorizing yourself with the internal traffic jams you create.

BROKEN PIECES

Ecclesiastes 3:11 tells us that, "...*God has made everything beautiful for its own time. He has planted eternity in the human heart, but even so, people cannot see the whole scope of God's work from beginning to end*" (NLT). When we are in the middle of a crisis, it is easy to panic because we are unable to see the whole scope of God's work from beginning to end. Many of us are guilty of immediately praying and telling God what the result should be and how He should get us there. Ecclesiastes 6:10 reveals that, "*Everything has already been decided. It was known long ago what each person would be. So, there is no use arguing with God about your destiny*" (NLT). This is telling us that we are wasting our time when we try to go our own way, do what we think is best, or try to fix a situation ourselves. God has a plan, and He knows what He's doing. I don't have all the answers, but I do know this: the very least that God can be to us is **GOOD**. He is a good God. Deuteronomy 32:4 declares, "*The Lord is the Rock, and His work is perfect! Yes, all His ways are right! God is true and faithful. He is good and honest*" (ERV). The work He does in your life is perfect. You can trust Him because He is good, and the result of what He is doing in your life will be good!

The question is… Can we really have peace amid our broken pieces? In Acts chapter twenty-seven we find Paul on his way to Rome to stand trial before Caesar. In verse seven and eight Paul says, "*We had several days of slow sailing, and after great difficulty we finally neared Cnidus. But the wind was against us, so we sailed across to Crete and along the sheltered coast of the island, past the cape of Salmone. We struggled along the coast with great difficulty and finally arrived at Fair Havens…*" (NLT). We all know about hard days and rough times. We know about times of difficulty. We know what it is like to feel as if the winds of life are against us. We know what it is like to struggle. Here is what I want you to get. On your way to peace, it doesn't have to be difficult, but it's not going to be easy. There is a wide range of options between difficult and easy. We tend to think that we only have two options – difficult or easy. Here are your other options: making it, doing it, hanging on, holding on, getting by, moving through, struggling, and growing. There are a lot of options between difficult and easy. To have peace among the broken pieces of our lives we must choose some other options. Which option do you choose?

Your peace posture will be determined by what you choose during the rough days. It will be determined by how you navigate yourself through the rough times. If you are going to deal with the frenzy and confusion, you're going to have a problem. If you remember to understand that it has already been decided and that the least God can be to you is good then you're going to look for peace first and then ask God, "How am I going to navigate through these difficult days and times of struggle?" Rather than asking God how you are going to make it and then panicking and making things harder than they should be by going your own way and trying to figure it out for yourself.

In Acts chapter twenty-seven they went through a difficult time, and they arrived at this place called, "Fair Haven". I want to ask you… How do you get to your "Fair Haven"? Your Fair Haven is the place where your broken pieces come together. The place where you turn away from your limitation and turn to God. How do you get there? Do you get there after much struggle? Or do you go there immediately? Sometimes you must help someone through their struggle in the middle of your struggle. That is what Paul finds himself having to do. He is headed to be put on trial and yet he is helping the people who are taking him there get through their storm. Sometimes that is how you get to your "Fair Haven" – investing in someone else.

In Acts chapter twenty-seven, they arrive at Fair Haven, but the captain of the ship had another destination in mind. We are all guilty of doing that. God brings us to one place, but we have another destination in mind. So, the captain decided he was going to move on from that place. Then Paul says in verse ten, "*'Men, I believe there is trouble ahead if we go on—shipwreck, loss of cargo, and danger to our lives as well.' But the officer in charge of the prisoners listened more to the ship's captain and the owner than to Paul. And since Fair Havens was an exposed harbor—a poor place to spend the winter—most of the crew wanted to go on to Phoenix, farther up the coast of Crete, and spend the winter there"* (NLT). This is just like us. We are always trying to get somewhere other than where we are right now. Don't get me wrong. We need to move forward in life, but sometimes we need to sit among our broken pieces, call a thing a thing, and do the work. We always want to know what or where the next place in life is and we want to try to force our way there when we haven't fully mastered where we are currently. We want to be somewhere other than where we are, but we have not experienced the full and abundant blessings of the place in which we are. We decide where we are is too hard and too uncomfortable, so we start wanting to drift, not knowing where we are going. We have no clear direction, but we want to drift. Drifting without a direction or purpose is what makes you lost – a lost soul. We must understand that the only way to peace is by staying connected to the source. When we start drifting, we are drifting away from the source. Jesus is our source. He is the Prince of Peace!

In Acts chapter twenty-seven they did not listen to Paul, and they went on their journey. Verse thirteen says, *"When a light wind began blowing from the south, the sailors thought they could make it. So, they pulled up anchor and sailed close to the shore of Crete. But the weather changed abruptly, and a wind of typhoon strength (called a "northeaster") burst across the island and blew us out to sea. The sailors couldn't turn the ship into the wind, so they gave up and let it run before the gale"* (NLT). Things got a little out of control. The winds started blowing. Things started abruptly changing. They lost control. So, they gave up. Sounds like you and me. As we read on, it tells us in verse eighteen, *"The next day, as gale-force winds continued to batter the ship, the crew began throwing the cargo overboard. The following day they even took some of the ship's gear and threw it overboard. The terrible storm raged for many days, blotting out the sun and the stars, until at last all hope was gone"* (NLT). **GOOD**! It is a good thing when all hope is gone, because that is when you finally turn to God. If there is some hope, you will continue to stand on your own. When you can see a way out, you will continue to stand on your own. When you think you can wiggle your way out of this situation or that situation, you will continue to stand on your own. Sometimes you must be shipwrecked and face the broken pieces so that you can really learn to trust God and let

Him lead you to peace. It doesn't matter what you throw overboard. You must be willing to be shipwrecked so God can lead you to peace.

The crew is facing a hopeless situation, and this is what Paul tells them in verse twenty-two, "*...take courage! None of you will lose your lives, even though the ship will go down. For last night an angel of the God to whom I belong and whom I serve stood beside me, and He said, 'Don't be afraid, Paul, for you will surely stand trial before Caesar! What's more,* **God in His goodness** *has granted safety to everyone sailing with you.' So, take courage! For I believe God. It will be just as He said. But we will be shipwrecked on an island*" (NLT). It does not matter that you are shipwrecked. You must remember this promise, "*...Do not be afraid and do not panic... For the LORD your God will personally go ahead of you. He will neither fail you nor abandon you*" (Deuteronomy 31:6, NLT). It does not matter that your spouse left you with a bunch of kids and a mortgage you can't afford. Don't be afraid! Don't panic! God has gone before you and He will never leave you nor forsake you! It doesn't matter how many pieces are broken around you, we must hold on to that Word. Because God in His goodness has granted you safety. Remember, the very least God can be to you is good!

In Acts chapter twenty-seven, when the morning dawned, they did not recognize the coastline. They saw a bay and they wondered if they could get between the rocks and get the ship safely to shore. The officers wanted to kill Paul because they blamed him for getting them into this mess. That's just like you and me. We blame somebody else for our problems. In verse forty-three it says, "*But the commanding officer wanted to spare Paul, so he didn't let them carry out their plan. Then he ordered all who could swim to jump overboard first and make for land. The others held on to planks or debris from the* **broken** *ship. So, everyone escaped safely to shore*" (NLT). They had to make it on the broken pieces. They had to use the broken piece to get to their place of peace. They had to grab on to whatever piece they could find and make it to safety. Sometimes you must do the same thing. In the middle of all your broken pieces, you grab on to one of them until you reach safety.

You can have peace in the broken pieces. You can rise above the broken pieces and stand on the promises of God. We must understand that even though the pieces are broken, God can make something out of nothing. That's what He did in the beginning. Genesis 1:2 states, *"The earth was formless and empty, and darkness covered the deep waters..."* (NLT). Now look at this beautiful world in which we live. God can take the broken pieces of your history, the broken pieces of your family, the broken pieces from you parents, the broken pieces of your heart, the broken pieces of your mind, the broken pieces from the places you keep putting yourself in, the broken pieces from the stuff the world throws at you, the broken pieces of your story, and He can use them for His glory and give you peace!

I don't know about you but there have been times that I felt like the boat I was in was shattered by storms. Your boat could be a dream, a marriage, a relationship, a career, or a goal and you look up and that thing is busted to pieces. Most of us look at that thing and say, "I can fix that." This is because we think we're in charge. Not only do we think we're in charge, but we think it is our right, our duty, and our responsibility to fix things, or change things, or make things different than they were. So here you are riding along in this dream, this marriage, this relationship, this career, or whatever your boat is, and you find yourself out in the middle of a storm and the storm starts beating it to pieces. Usually, the first thing to go is our knowledge. We forget everything we have seen God do, all that He has promised, all that He has given us and equipped us with, and the truth that is in His Word. We start walking in fear and panic. This causes the second thing to leave us, which is faith. We start feeling like we are out there in the middle of the sea on a sinking boat by ourselves just like the disciples in Mark 4:35-41. When they remembered that Jesus was in the boat with them and they turned to Him, He spoke, "Peace! Be still!" in the middle of their brokenness. We must turn from our limitations and turn to Him. Jesus didn't stop there. Then He looked at them and said, "Why are you so fearful? How is it that you have no faith?". This is because they had the power to find peace in the middle of their brokenness. Instead, they walked in fear and forgetfulness.

I want to encourage you today. I don't know what broken pieces you may be living with. It may be brokenness from your childhood, brokenness from a failed marriage or relationship, brokenness from a failed business or career. Whatever your brokenness is, you can find peace in the middle of all the broken pieces.

YOU CAN HAVE PEACE IN THE MIDDLE OF THE BROKEN PIECES.

Sometimes we must have the pieces broken up and broken open so that we can see a new way. A new vision will be birthed and grow from the brokenness! When you come through a hard time you gain a new perspective. When you come through a bad situation, you come out and look at yourself and realize you are greater than you think you are. Because greater is He that is in you than he that is in the world (1 John 4:4).

Moving to peace from broken pieces is understanding that even when you go through the fire, you will not be burned. It is turning from your limited humanness to the almighty power of God that is all around you continually calling you higher, beckoning you to another way of being, and asking you to stand above the broken pieces. It is turning from your limited humanness and turning to the Almighty God who is in you. It's a choice! You get to choose to be broken and broke down or you choose to be whole and holy. You can choose to stand courageously and say, "I will not fear. I will not back down. I will not give up. No matter how hard the winds are blowing. I'm going to grab on to a piece of debris and I am going to float my way to something bigger and something better!" It doesn't matter that the storm is raging all around you! Why? Because the ocean that you are in, God made it! If you are currently in a storm, Jesus is there with you! If you are currently in a fiery trial, you are not alone! You can have peace during brokenness! It does not matter if your child has lost their mind, or your spouse walked out on you, or your career is on the rocks, or your finances are out of control. It does not matter what the doctor's report is. It does not matter what it looks like. It does not matter how hopeless it may seem. You can have peace during the broken pieces! It does not matter who turned their back on you. It does not matter that your parents rejected you! It does not matter what level of education you have! It does not matter that you come from poverty. It does not matter that they raped you or abused you. You can have peace during the broken pieces. Allow God to change your perception and focus. He will help you take those pieces and build something beautiful. He will help you take those pieces and build something that will take you higher. Get on your knees, humble yourself, submit your attention and your intention to Him, surrender your life, your past, your present, and your future to Him. I knew a woman who had a child that was living out of order. She asked me to pray for God to save her son. I stood in agreement with her for God to get her son off the streets and to save him. She called me a few weeks later and said, "Our prayers didn't work. My son was arrested, and he's going to jail." I asked her, "What did you ask me to pray for?" She said, "For God to get my son off the streets and to save him." I said, "Then why are you complaining and not praising? God has answered your prayer." She couldn't believe my response! She was so offended. Now her son is out of jail. While he was in jail he got saved and started studying the Word of God. Now he works in ministry, ministering to youth. Look at God! That was a broken piece in her life. Look at what God did with it!

We must learn to trust God with our broken pieces. We may not always understand the process, but I assure you, His plan is better than ours. God said in Jeremiah 29:11, ' *"For I know the plans I have for you," says the Lord. "They are plans for good and not for disaster, to give you a future and a hope"'* (NLT). If we say we believe this scripture, then we need to change our perception and focus and learn to trust God even when we don't understand the process or can't see a way through. Don't worry about the outcome, because we have the promise in Jeremiah 29:11 that it is going to be **GOOD!** I don't know what you're facing today but I know this: God has new relationships for you, and they are going to be **GOOD!** God has a new job for you, and it is going to be **GOOD!** God has a new car for you, and it is going to be **GOOD!** I encourage you to not wait for the end result, start praising right now. Praise God on credit. Praise Him in advance. Don't wait for your promise to be fulfilled, start thanking Him right now!

ROCK BOTTOM

You may be reading this right now and feel like you're at rock bottom. That place where you have nothing left to lose. The place where you could go no lower. That could be mentally, physically, or emotionally. Rock bottom is different for everyone. For some it is a health challenge. For others it's a divorce. For someone else it could be a financial trouble. I have good news! Rock bottom has a purpose in our lives… if we're willing to see it differently.

When people hit rock bottom, they want out quickly. That's not the purpose of rock bottom. Most people are not taught how to face life's challenges. Which means, they don't have the needed tools. Some of us gain the tools we need through trial and error. When we are facing rock bottom, it is important for us to remember that it is God who created the rock! In fact, God is the rock. Which means there is a plan, a purpose, something greater and grander for you. Deuteronomy 32:4 declares, "**The Lord is the Rock**, *and His work is perfect! Yes, all His ways are right! God is true and faithful. He is good and honest*" (ERV). Here are the gifts you can get from the rock…

1. **The rock stops you from falling.** When you have hit rock bottom, you can't go any further.

2. **The rock is usually painful enough to motivate us to change.** Unfortunately, we humans must begin experiencing pain before we are willing to change. Things must get uncomfortable or really scary before we will consider making necessary changes.

3. **The rock is a firm foundation you can build upon.** If you can just get yourself to stop feeling sorry and afraid, if you can stop the complaining and worrying, you can build on the rock.

4. **There is only one direction to go from rock bottom… UP!** When you have hit rock bottom you don't have to wonder about what direction you should go in. Start looking up – to the Father. Start moving up – to your next.

The **ROCK** stands for **R**emoving **O**bstacles **C**onsciously **K**nowing better is possible. The rock teaches us where we are weak and where we need to be strengthened. The rock shows us what we need to remove from our lives. The rock helps us to know that better is ahead of us. Let's talk about the bottom. Because when we think of the "bottom" we think of something bad or negative. The **BOTTOM** stands for **B**eing **O**bedient, **T**ransforming **T**hinking, **O**pen to **M**iracles. Be obedient to God and His Word. Transform your thinking from negative to positive, from fear to courage, from doubt to faith, from bitterness to joy, from anger to peace, and from hurt to forgiveness. When we start being obedient and we start transforming our thinking, we open ourselves up for miracles to take place. Things start to change and turn around in our lives.

How do you get **OUT** of rock bottom? It's simple. **O**wn, **U**nderstand, and **T**rust. You need to **own** that you contributed to your arrival at rock bottom. We must be willing to ask the question and find the answer to, "How did I contribute to my getting here?" What have you denied, resisted, ignored, or avoided that got you here? You must stop blaming others for the reason you are where you are. Stop telling the sad story. Stop thinking about what "they" did or what "they" said. You must stop denying that you are where you are, which is rock bottom. Own it. It is not happening to you. It is happening through you. Here is the great news, it is happening for you! You not only need to own it, but you need to **understand** that rock bottom does not have to be your destination. You can go higher. A new level is available to you. Understand that there is something for you to learn from where you are and what you are going through. Understand that if you don't learn what you need to learn, you will find yourself at rock bottom all over again. Not only do you need to own it and understand it, but you need to **trust** God through the process. It's not easy, and it's painful, but God is with you, and He is for you every step of the way. Remember, God created the rock. He is the rock. He will use it for your good. In Romans 8:28 the Apostle Paul says, "*...we know that God causes everything to work together for the good of those who love God and are called according to His purpose for them*" (NLT). Trust that God will use this to grow, heal, and stretch you into your "better" and into peace. Remember, we need to let go of resistance. **O**wn, **u**nderstand, and **t**rust rock bottom.

MAINTAINING YOUR PEACE

The psalmist stated in Psalm 34:12-14, "*Does anyone want to live a life that is long and prosperous? Then keep your tongue from speaking evil and your lips from telling lies! Turn away from evil and do good. Search for peace, and* **work to maintain it**" (NLT). If we want to enjoy our lives, we must tell the truth, search for peace, and work to maintain peace. The way we work to maintain our peace is to take small steps towards it every day. Here are a few ways we can develop a peaceful lifestyle...

WE
MUST
MAKE
PEACE
A PRIORITY.

———————————————

1. Be selective with how you spend your time. Proverbs 21:5 says, "*Good planning and hard work lead to prosperity, but hasty shortcuts lead to poverty*" (NLT). You may be trying to do too many things and end up doing none of them well. Trying to do a lot of "stuff" and hurrying trying to get it all done is the flesh trying to do more than the Holy Spirit is leading us to do. We need to be led by the Spirit in what we choose to do and how we spend our time. Galatians 5:16-17 and 22-23 says, "*So, I say, let the Holy Spirit guide your lives. Then you will not be doing what your sinful nature* (the flesh) *craves. The sinful nature wants to fulfill its desires, which is just the opposite of what the Spirit wants. And the Spirit gives us desires that are the opposite of what the sinful nature desires. These two forces* (the flesh and the Spirit) *are constantly fighting each other, so you are not free to carry out your good intentions.* (Because what we want to do may be a good idea but not a God idea.) *The Holy Spirit produces this kind of fruit in our lives: love, joy,* **peace***, patience, kindness, goodness, faithfulness, gentleness, and self-control*" (NLT).

2. Resist procrastination. God's Word tells us to exercise SELF-discipline. We are given this wisdom in Proverbs 13:4, "*Lazy people want much but get little, but those who work hard will prosper*" (NLT). We need to do what we know we need to do **NOW** so we can fully enjoy our times of rest. Hebrews 12:11 teaches us that, "*No discipline* (Whether it come from others or us.) *is enjoyable while it is happening — It's painful! But afterward there will be a peaceful harvest of right living for those who are trained in this way*" (NLT). Sitting on the couch relaxing sounds wonderful, but you can never truly enjoy it when you know you have a list of things that need to be done. So, don't procrastinate. Get it done and then enjoy your relaxation time.

3. Set appropriate boundaries for interruptions. We read in Mark 6:31, "*Jesus and His followers were in a very busy place. There were so many people that He and His followers did not even have time to eat. He said to them, "Come with Me. We will go to a quiet place to be alone. There we will get some rest*"" (NLT). Jesus basically said, "Let's go find some peace!" Life is busy and full of interruptions. So many notifications ringing on our phones and computers. Phone calls, text messages, social media notifications, and emails are all trying to get our attention. We must learn to set boundaries that help us manage our peace. For example: Be like Jesus.

Schedule times when you are "off limits". Schedule time to get by yourself or with those you love and give yourself a break. You deserve it. You need it.

4. Pray and be thankful. The Apostle Paul said, *"Do not worry about anything; instead, pray about everything. Tell God what you need and thank Him for all He has done"* (Philippians 4:6, NLT). Instead of trying to control everything in your life, **PRAY**! Instead of trying to figure everything out on your own, **PRAY**! Instead of trying to make things happen in your life, **PRAY**! When your mind is troubled, remember all God has done for you and thank Him. When you feel worried, remember how God has turned it around for you in the past and thank Him. When anxiety concerning your situation hits, remember how God came through for you before and thank Him. We read in Philippians 4:7, *"Then you will experience God's peace, which exceeds anything we can understand. His peace will guard your hearts and minds as you live in Christ Jesus"* (NLT). His peace will guard our hearts and minds from believing the lies of the enemy that say, "You will not make it!" "It will never change!" "It is hopeless!"

We must make peace a priority, take practical steps towards maintaining peace, and let God lead us every day into His perfect peace that passes all understanding.

LET IT GO

I don't know what your "thing" is. It may be a bad habit, addiction, fear, anxiety, unhealthy relationships, negative mindsets, etc. Regardless of what your "thing" is you can live in freedom. You can live in peace not pieces. Choose today to call that "thing" what it really is, expose it, deal with it, and let it go. I understand all too well that letting go is hard work. When I'm upset or worried, sometimes it seems impossible to let "it" go. If we are honest, many times we don't want to let go. Here's what you do when you can't seem to let it go…

1. **Train Your Mind.** The yearning, missing, wanting, or feeling bad is a function of the mind and not of the heart or of the soul. There may be a thought or a train of thoughts you are holding that have you stuck. There is something you are telling yourself about that person or that "thing" that is not grounded in truth. It is grounded in a lack of self-value. It is grounded in codependence. Train your mind to focus on the truth, not what your emotions are telling you. You train your mind by pausing, taking a deep breath, and then changing the thought. It is just that easy. When you are trying to let go, be mindful not to think about the why, the what, the who, or the how. Put a stop to toxic thoughts. Refuse them. Don't allow your mind to think any thought that leads you down a path of suffering. Be mindful to focus on the truth: you are loved, you do have purpose, you can succeed, there is more for you than against you, you will be okay, you can do this, you can choose to let go, you can be free, peace is yours, and your best is yet to come! Be mindful and choose to think on these truths. You are not obligated to think, ponder, or entertain every little thought that knocks on the door of your mind.

2. **Be Grateful.** Instead of focusing on what you are missing or what you no longer have. Be grateful for what you do have and for what is coming to your life. Be grateful for your next. Be grateful for the experience of where you have come from and what you have gone through. Smile about it. Laugh about it. Be grateful for it. When you choose to be grateful, more comes in your direction.

3. **Do Not Deny It and Do Not Give It Control.** Do not deny that the part of you that wants to hold on to that person or that "thing" exists. Feelings buried alive do not die. They erupt and corrupt the soul. So, acknowledge it. Acknowledge that it's there. Then make it obey. Make it obey the choice to let go. Make it obey the choice to go forward. Make it obey the choice to be free. Don't let the desire to hold on to that person or that "thing" control you, your freedom, or your future.

You hold the key to your freedom. You can let go. You must choose to stop being the abused, abandoned, and rejected little girl or boy. You must choose to stop being a victim. The choice is yours. Your parent may have failed you, abandoned you, rejected you, and denied you. That is the truth. Here is the other truth: you do not need that parent to become the man or woman you were created to be. You have a choice. You get to choose to not fail, abandon, reject, or deny yourself. Your past may be full of missteps and negative circumstances or experiences that happened in your life. That is the truth. Here is the other truth: you are not a victim of your past. Do not provide your past the power to determine your future! You are a pioneer of your future. Your past does not determine your future and where you have been does not determine where you are going. Learn to let it go and let yourself grow! You must let go of your past season so you can embrace your new season. This does not mean the past season was bad. It just means you must make room for all the "new" God wants to do in your life! If you want to walk in peace, you must understand that the experiences that you have had are just that, experiences. They are not who you are, and they do not determine the course of your life. So don't give them that power.

VOTE FOR YOU

The one thing that you have that nobody else has is **YOU**! Your voice. Your mind. Your story. Your vision. Your gifts. Even if others don't see your value and overlook your worth - write, draw, build, plan, play, dance, sing, and live as only **YOU** can. You are an incredible force God has placed on the earth! He has more for you! So, vote for you…

If it costs you your peace it is too expensive. Let it go. Make peace a priority. Sometimes you must avoid certain people, places, conversations, or situations to protect your mental, emotional, and spiritual state. Protect your peace. It's okay to cancel. It's okay to not answer a phone call or text. It's okay to want to be alone. It's okay to take a day off. It's okay to do nothing. It's okay to speak up. It's okay to let go.

Decide what you are and are not going to tolerate in your life. Then draw a line. Don't draw a line and then when it is crossed back up and draw another line. No! Set clear boundaries and stick to them. You train people how to treat you. You can choose what is or is not allowed in your life. Do not compromise for someone else at the expense of your joy or peace. Your feelings matter. So, vote for you! When the enemy comes in like a flood, we want the Lord to raise a standard against him. Set the standard. God will not raise a standard that does not exist.

If it is out of your hands, it deserves freedom from your mind too. You are not in control. God is. Choose to trust Him. In Proverbs 3:5-6 we are instructed to, *"Trust in the Lord with all your heart; do not depend on your own understanding. Seek His will in all you do, and He will show you which path to take"* (NLT). Do not depend on you or your own warped understanding. Seek the One who is in control of all things and will lead you down the path to peace.

You have a right to peace in your life. Focus on the good in your life and celebrate it. Do not beat yourself up. Do not hold on to the broken pieces. You have a reason to live in peace because stress makes you ugly and unattractive! I don't know about you, but I don't want to hold on to anything that makes me look ugly. You have a responsibility to be a demonstration of peace to the world. Follow the process. Call a "thing" a "thing". Tell the truth. Start healing. Remember, healing hurts. It must hurt before it can heal, but once it starts to heal you don't remember the pain.

I declare over your life now...
YOU WILL WALK IN PEACE NOT PIECES!

TWELVE

STOP BEING STUCK

...Stand up, pick up your mat, and walk!
John 5:8 (NLT)

Many of us are stuck. We are stuck in a mindset. We are stuck in an attitude. We are stuck on rejection and denial. We are stuck in a belief system. We are stuck on the past. We are stuck on a failure or mistake. We are stuck on what "they" said or did. We are stuck in a relationship. We are stuck on stupid decisions. We are stuck on our excuses. We are just stuck. We must choose to draw a line in our lives, step over the line, and choose what we are leaving behind.

You don't have to be stuck. You really can release it, let it go, and move forward. All you need to do is get up and walk. That's right. Just get up and walk away. Walk away from the broken, poor, defeated, and depressed mindsets. Walk away from the bad, nasty, wrong attitudes. Walk away from the belief system you were taught as a child. Walk away from the unhealthy relationship. Walk away from the stupid, dumb decisions. Just walk away! Walk away and pursue a new mindset, attitude, belief system, relationship, or decision. There is more for you! Stop praying for God to be a genie in a bottle and face yourself, face the truth! Your family, your friends, and your future will be glad you did!

Breakthrough happens when you confront what isn't right in your life. God did not create you to be scared. He did not create you to be broken. He did not create you to be addicted. He did not create you to be mean and hateful. He did not create you to suffer or struggle. He created you to be fruitful and multiply! Here is the question… what fruit are you producing? Because the fruit you produce, multiplies in your life. If you produce rotten fruit such as negativity, bad decisions, unhealthy relationships, addiction, etc. those things begin to multiply in your life, and they are passed down from generation to generation.

For God to do or give us something new, He must disrupt something normal.

We must do the same thing. For example, normally when we hear, "**NO**" we start wasting our time giving CPR to dead situations. We get stuck on "**NO**". Try this. When you hear a "**NO**", learn to think, "**NEXT**". Start seeking what God has next for your life instead of trying to force your way and make something happen. Stop sitting and waiting around hoping for a "**NO**" to become a "**YES**". There is more for you, but you must do the work.

NO MORE EXCUSES

In John chapter five we find the story of a man who was stuck. John 5:2-4 states, *"Inside the city, near the Sheep Gate, was the pool of Bethesda, with five covered porches. Crowds of sick people—blind, lame, or paralyzed—lay on the porches, waiting for a certain movement of the water, for an angel of the Lord came from time to time and stirred up the water. And the first person to step in after the water was stirred was healed of whatever disease he had"* (NLT). We are all guilty of hanging out at the pool of Bethesda. We hang out with people who are blind and have no vision for their future. We hang out with people who are lame, uninspired, and dull. We hang out with people who are paralyzed and incapable of moving forward into purpose and destiny. We hang out with people who are paralyzed and unable to think or act because of panic and fear. We hang out at the pool of Bethesda, sitting around on our "porch of do nothing" just waiting for our turn - waiting for God to come down and do all the work.

So, all these sick people are lying around on the porches at the pool of Bethesda and verse five tells us that one of the men lying there had been sick for thirty-eight years. This sounds like you and me. We walk around all our lives holding on and stuck in mindsets, attitudes, relationships, cycles, breakdowns, beliefs, pain, addictions, fears, and other worthless stuff. We carry it around like we are going to win an award for it. When God got off His throne and He hung on the cross, He said, **"IT IS FINISHED!"** Why? He said it so that you would not have to be stuck! What do I mean? I mean, for your anxiety, it is finished! For your depression, it is finished! For your brokenness, it is finished! For your addiction, it is finished! For the ugly divorce you had to walk through, it is finished! For your kid who is strung out on drugs, it is finished! For the infertility you have been diagnosed with, it is finished! For the cancer diagnosis, it is finished! For the hopeless situation, it is finished!

For thirty-eight years the man sat on his porch of "do nothing". Look at what happens in John 5:6, *"When Jesus saw him and knew he had been ill for a long time, he asked him, "Would you like to get well?" "* (NLT). Let me ask you… would you like to get well? Would you like to get unstuck? Would you like to be whole? Would you like to be free? Look at the man's response in John 5:7, *"'I can't, sir," the sick man said, "for I have no one to put me into the pool when the water bubbles up. Someone else always gets there ahead of me" "* (NLT). His response sounds like our response. We say, "Woe is me!" and we give all our little excuses as to why we are not well yet. We explain why we are stuck. We list every excuse we can as to why we are not whole or free. Read this very carefully…

Breakthrough begins where our excuses end. Stop making excuses. Stop complaining. Stop accepting where you're at. Do the work!

Check out Jesus' response to the man in John 5:8, *"Jesus told him, "Stand up, pick up your mat, and walk!" "* (NLT). This is God's response to all your excuses today. He is asking, "Are you done? Are you ready to get

BREAKTHROUGH BEGINS WHERE OUR EXCUSES END.

---

up and help yourself? Are you ready to break the victim mindset off you? You need to get up and walk!" So do that today. Get up and walk!

What were the results? In John 5:9 we read, *"Instantly, the man was healed! He rolled up his sleeping mat and began walking!"* (NLT). If you will stop sitting in your sad story. If you will stop sitting in your bad attitude. If you will stop sitting in your defeated mindset, broken spirit, and all your excuses. If you will pick up your mat and walk, or in other words, do the work. You will find healing, breakthrough, freedom, and victory! Stop allowing your problems to be your prison. Stop being loyal to mistakes. Stop believing your excuses. Do the work and walk away from whatever you are stuck in. The choice is yours.

STAND UP. PICK UP YOUR MAT. WALK.

In John chapter five, verse eight, Jesus tells the man at the pool of Bethesda to stand up, pick up his mat, and walk. If you are feeling stuck today, it's just that simple… Stand up, pick up your mat, and walk.

Stand Up. Instead of accepting where you are in life, stand up! Instead of accepting defeat, stand up! Instead of accepting the same ole sad story you keep telling yourself, stand up! Stand up for your future! Stand up for your breakthrough! Stand up for your healing and peace! Stand up for your family! Stand up for who God has called you to be and what He has called you to do! Stand up.

Pick Up Your Mat. Instead of sitting around waiting for something to change. Pick up your mat, or in other words, do the work! Pick up the broken pieces of your life and keep going. Don't stop, quit, or give up. It's painful. It's not fun, but it is necessary. Doing the work is confronting those things that keep you from being the best of who you are and living the best life God has for you. It can make you uneasy and uncomfortable, but it will make you better.

Walk. Walk away. You do not have to stay where you are or where you have been. If you have parked there, it's because you chose to park there. Make the choice to simply walk away. That's okay. The dysfunction and excuses we make up will try to convince us that it's not safe to walk away because being broke, busted, and disgusted is all we have ever known. It's comfortable. I challenge you to get uncomfortable. Walk out from the dysfunction and the excuses. Walk in the plan, purpose, and power God has for you.

Galatians 5:1 says, *"Christ has set us free to live a free life. So take your stand! Never again let anyone put a harness of slavery on you"* (MSG). If you do not feel free, you are living beneath your privilege. Jesus paid the price for your freedom from it all. So live free. Stand up for that freedom, peace, joy, and wholeness. Stand up for it and then do the work to maintain it. You must do the work because the devil will do his best to take it from you and your flesh will sabotage it every time.

If you're going to walk in all that God has for you, you're going to have to stand up for it and work to keep it. Just like the children of Israel when they reached the promise land, once they took possession of it, the work was not done. They had to defend it and protect it. What God has for you is yours, which means it is your responsibility. If you end up back in the wilderness, it is no one's fault but your own.

TELL THE TRUTH

We want God to fix things without us having to do anything. We all have our conditions. We all have our "thing". Some of us can hide it easier than others. Do not be ashamed and do not feel guilty. Jesus endured the cross to defeat shame and guilt. Shame and guilt are what tell you to hide that "thing".

We all have a "thing". Expose it! Call it what it really is. Don't try to paint another picture or cover it up with duct tape or a band aid. Tell the truth! Because duct tape does not fix it and a band aid does not heal it.

Jesus did not ask the man at the pool of Bethesda, "Do you want **IT** to change?" He asked him, "Do **YOU** want to change?" He didn't ask him, "Do you want **IT** to get better?" He asked him, "Do **YOU** want to get well?" Dealing with your "thing" starts with **YOU**.

You cannot change what you will not challenge. You cannot challenge what you will not confront.

Confront your excuses. Confront your sad story. Tell the truth. Call a thing a thing. It should not feel comfortable. It should not be easy. If it is, you're not doing right.

Calling a "thing" a "thing" is something we all must do in our lives if we are ever truly going to live free. Jesus said in John 8:32, *You will know the truth, and the truth will make you free*" (ERV). Remember, when you choose to look right at a "thing", acknowledge its existence, call it exactly by its name, and then decide what role it will play in your life, you have just chosen to take the first step toward freedom.

I want you to always remember this...
Honesty is the place where breakthrough happens.
So, tell the truth.

ACKNOWLEDGEMENTS
THANK YOU!

They say that it takes a village to raise a child. Well… it took a village to make the "Call A Thing A Thing" book a reality! I am so blessed to have so many people in my life who have helped me on the seven-year journey to completing this book. There have been so many friends and family who have encouraged me along the way. So many who have helped keep me honest and call a thing a thing in my own life.

Olivia Aziz – You inspire me every day! Your support and encouragement in ministry help me keep going. I love you and I love doing life with you!

Veronica Perez – Thank you so much for the time spent to read and re-read my book. Your feedback means so much to me!

Pastor Oleda Atkinson Ratchford – Thank you so much for the time spent to edit and review my book. You are a general in the faith and I am honored to receive your feedback!

Metro Tab Church Family – Thank you so much for loving and supporting me and my family! You are a source of strength in our lives!

Dr. Steve & Reita Ball – Thank you for loving me and supporting me for so many years! You have allowed me to stand on your shoulders and go higher.

Gaber & Sherry Aziz, Dillard & Imogene Davis – You have been more than parents and grandparents. You have been examples in my life. You have taught me to aim high, work hard, and never give up. You have given me a firm foundation to stand on and build my life on. I love you and I thank you!

ABOUT THE AUTHOR
ADAM AZIZ

Adam Aziz currently lives in Chattanooga, TN with his wife, Olivia, and their son, Axel. They serve as the Executive Pastors of Worship and Ministries at Metro Tab Church, a Spirit-filled, diverse, non-denominational church.

Adam comes from a rich history of spirit-filled pastors and church leaders. From a young age Adam has used his gifts to serve the local church through leading worship, serving in youth and children's ministry, administration, hospitality, and many other areas of ministry.

Adam and his wife, Olivia, house a unique, soul-filled, and Spirit-led sound that stirs the hearts of listeners from all walks of life. They both have a firm family foundation and a strong Pentecostal background. They carry a spirit of unity for the body of Christ and they love God, family, church, and all of God's people fiercely and relentlessly!

Adam is fueled by a passion concerning character building, faith, and destiny living. His ministry is marked by God's resilient passion for people and His desire to equip and empower them to live godly lives. Whether it is through Adam's singing, speaking, or writing – people from all walks of life are inspired and provoked to pursue a life of integrity, to "re-think" faith, and to love themselves and others more. Adam's desire is for people to come to the realization that with God's grace, nothing is impossible. Above all else, Adam wants to see people find a lasting relationship with Jesus.

LEARN MORE

Check out other resources, blogs, books, music, apparel, accessories, and more from Adam & Olivia Aziz

WWW.ADAMANDOLIVIA.COM

NOTES

CHAPTER 2

Merriam-Webster. (n.d.). Work. In Merriam-Webster.com dictionary. Retrieved April 27, 2022, from https://www.merriam-webster.com/dictionary/work

Merriam-Webster. (n.d.). Prune. In Merriam-Webster.com dictionary. Retrieved April 27, 2022, from https://www.merriam-webster.com/dictionary/prune

Merriam-Webster. (n.d.). Abide. In Merriam-Webster.com dictionary. Retrieved April 27, 2022, from https://www.merriam-webster.com/dictionary/abide

Merriam-Webster. (n.d.). Process. In Merriam-Webster.com dictionary. Retrieved April 27, 2022, from https://www.merriam-webster.com/dictionary/process

CHAPTER 6

Merriam-Webster. (n.d.). Possess. In Merriam-Webster.com dictionary. Retrieved May 2, 2022, from https://www.merriam-webster.com/dictionary/possess

CHAPTER 7

Merriam-Webster. (n.d.). Righteous. In Merriam-Webster.com dictionary. Retrieved May 4, 2022, from https://www.merriam-webster.com/dictionary/righteous

CHAPTER 8

Merriam-Webster. (n.d.). Vice. In Merriam-Webster.com dictionary. Retrieved May 4, 2022, from https://www.merriam-webster.com/dictionary/vice

CHAPTER 10

Merriam-Webster. (n.d.). Reasoning. In Merriam-Webster.com dictionary. Retrieved May 10, 2022, from https://www.merriam-webster.com/dictionary/reasoning

Merriam-Webster. (n.d.). Anxiety. In Merriam-Webster.com dictionary. Retrieved May 10, 2022, from https://www.merriam-webster.com/dictionary/anxiety

Merriam-Webster. (n.d.). Worry. In Merriam-Webster.com dictionary. Retrieved May 10, 2022, from https://www.merriam-webster.com/dictionary/worry

9 780578 282763